I0202768

UNMASKING NARCISSISM

Kenza Haddock, LPCS, BCPC

UNMASKING NARCISSISM by Kenza Haddock, LPCS, BCPC
Published by Charisma House, an imprint of Charisma Media
1150 Greenwood Blvd., Lake Mary, Florida 32746

statistics and other data are constantly updated. Neither the publisher nor the author assumes any responsibility for errors or for changes that occur after publication. Further, the publisher and author do not have any control over and do not assume any responsibility for third-party websites or their content.

For more resources like this, visit MyCharismaShop.com and the author's website at kenzahaddock.com.

Cataloging-in-Publication Data is on file with the Library of Congress.
International Standard Book Number: 978-1-63641-391-4
E-book ISBN: 978-1-63641-392-1

1 2025
Printed in the United States of America

Most Charisma Media products are available at special quantity discounts for bulk purchase for sales promotions, premiums, fund-raising, and educational needs. For details, call us at (407) 333-0600 or visit our website at www.charismamedia.com.

People and names in this book are composites created by the author from her experiences as a mental health professional. Names and details of their stories have been changed, and any similarity between the names and stories of individuals described in this book and individuals known to readers is purely coincidental.

To God be the glory!

I have learned to kiss the wave that throws me against the Rock of Ages.

—Charles Spurgeon

CONTENTS

Introduction

WHY NARCISSISM?

NARCISSISTIC ABUSE CAN be one of the most psychologically devastating forms of abuse, especially because it often targets one's identity and reality. It creates a soul-crushing, heart-aching, and mind-boggling confusion within you. It's common for a person who fell into the trap of a narcissist to spend weeks, months, and at times even years trying to reconstruct the sequence of events that led up to the abuse in order to make sense of the pain they experienced or are experiencing—only to find themselves back to square one, without closure, rationale, or sense of peace.

Through the years, dozens of books have been published on the topic of narcissism. After consulting with and treating patients who have experienced narcissistic abuse, I've come to find that though many books give great information on this topic, not one book in the market points to the true origin of narcissistic abuse and equips you with biblical and clinical strategies to live a lifestyle that overcomes narcissistic abuse and repels narcissists from your life. This book provides you with that.

As a trauma counselor, it's common for me to treat patients who have dealt with multiple narcissists in their lives and who, after seeking treatment elsewhere, ended up feeling defenseless against the endless cycle of abuse—and ultimately defeated. If this feeling resonates with you, this book is for you.

Unmasking Narcissism is descriptive, prescriptive, and preventive: *descriptive* in that it explains the true biblical roots of narcissistic abuse so you can stop pushing away the right people while gravitating toward the wrong ones in your life; *prescriptive* in that it gives you the exact tools you need to eradicate narcissistic abuse from your life; and *preventive* in that you will receive two powerful principles that when applied will ward off any narcissist who tries to set foot into your life.

I encourage you to journal your thoughts to the questions and prompts throughout this book. If needed, you can use the space for journaling at the back of the book.

Make It Personal

What is one problem you'd like to resolve through reading this book?

I'm grateful for the time you've decided to invest in your life. I can't wait to hear how God has used this material to transform you and strengthen you from the inside out!

PART I
NARCISSISM UNVEILED

Chapter 1

THE ORIGINAL NARCISSIST

A LONG, LONG TIME ago, before God created Adam and Eve, the Bible says God created the world (Gen. 1:1), and He called His creation good (v. 25). His created order included angels who glorify the Lord day and night. One of those angels was named Lucifer, the angel of light. One day Lucifer, who held a high position in heaven, set out to take over God's throne and be like God. Isaiah 14:12–15 provides a symbolic description of Lucifer's fall:

> How you have fallen from heaven, morning star, son of the dawn! You have been cast down to the earth, you who once laid low the nations! You said in your heart, "I will ascend to the heavens; I will raise my throne above the stars of God; I will sit enthroned on the mount of assembly, on the

> utmost heights of Mount Zaphon. I will ascend above the tops of the clouds; I will make myself like the Most High." But you are brought down to the realm of the dead, to the depths of the pit.

Since God is all-knowing and all-powerful, Lucifer's plan failed. Satan's pride led to his fall from God's grace and his loss of the prominent position he had been awarded by God. In Luke 10:18 Jesus describes Satan's fall by saying, "I saw Satan fall like lightning from heaven." If this wasn't bad enough, during his fall Satan didn't go down by himself. The Bible shows that when his plan to take over God's throne failed, Satan deceived one-third of heaven's angels toward rebellion, leading to their fall as well. Revelation 12:3–4 describes this account as follows:

> Then another sign appeared in heaven: an enormous red dragon with seven heads and ten horns and seven crowns on its heads. Its tail swept a third of the stars out of the sky and flung them to the earth. The dragon stood in front of the woman who was about to give birth, so that it might devour her child the moment he was born.

Thousands of years later those fallen angels, also known as demons, continue to conduct their master's bidding.

After causing the fall of a third of heaven's angels, Satan turned to God's most precious possessions next and decided to take them down with him as well. This brings us to the creation of mankind. Genesis 1:27 says,

"So God created man in his own image, in the image of God he created them; male and female he created them." God, the Creator, made Adam and Eve to live under His authority in a close, loving relationship with Him. The Bible shows that when God made Adam and Eve, He gave them a sense of identity.

> And God blessed them. And God said to them, "Be fruitful and multiply and fill the earth and subdue it, and have dominion over the fish of the sea and over the birds of the heavens and over every living thing that moves on the earth."
>
> —Genesis 1:28–29, esv

Not only did God give them an identity; He gave them authority and freedom to exercise it within the boundaries of His will. God also drew a boundary line around the tree of the knowledge of good and evil. He told Adam not to eat from it, as well as the consequences that would result from doing so.

Then entered Satan, whose name means "deceiver." Satan knew that Adam and Eve's position was directly connected to their relationship with God. So to destroy them, he knew he had to separate them from Him. To do so, he employed what I refer to as the *cycle of destruction*. Let's walk through it.

The Cycle of Destruction

Step 1: Deception

Genesis 3:1–4 says,

> Now the serpent was more crafty than any of the wild animals the Lord God had made. He said to the woman, "Did God really say, 'You must not eat from any tree in the garden'?" The woman said to the serpent, "We may eat fruit from the trees in the garden, but God did say, 'You must not eat fruit from the tree that is in the middle of the garden, and you must not touch it, or you will die.'" "You will not certainly die," the serpent said to the woman.

Deception is often initiated by the perpetrator, who in this case was Satan. Deception is meant to confuse you to the point where you question the reality before your eyes.

Step 2: Doubt

When Eve turned her attention to Satan, he used it as an opportunity to induce doubt about God's intention toward her and Adam. Genesis 3:4–5 states, "'You will not certainly die,' the serpent said to the woman. 'For God knows that when you eat from it your eyes will be opened, and you will be like God, knowing good and evil.'" Up to this point, Eve had spent time with God. She knew Him intimately, so her red flags should have been going off because the way Satan described Him wasn't congruent with who He is.

Step 3: Disobedience

Entertaining Satan's words and choosing to believe him led to Eve directly disobeying what God said not to do. Genesis 3:4–6 says,

> When the woman saw that the fruit of the tree was good for food and pleasing to the eye, and also desirable for gaining wisdom, she took some and ate it. She also gave some to her husband, who was with her, and he ate it.

As we see from Genesis 3:4–6, Satan managed to deceive Eve into believing she would surely not die just from eating fruit from a tree. He convinced Eve that the negative repercussions God warned about for disobeying Him would not come to pass and that God was holding something back from her—and didn't have her best interests at heart. Thus, he deceived her into the very trap he had set out for her. Satan didn't have to go to Adam with the same lie; he instead used Eve to lead her husband into the trap.

Step 4: Dread

Genesis 3:7–8 recalls once Adam and Eve disobeyed God,

> The eyes of both of them were opened, and they realized they were naked; so they sewed fig leaves together and made coverings for themselves. Then the man and his wife heard the sound of the LORD God as he was walking in the garden in the

> cool of the day, and they hid from the LORD God among the trees of the garden.

Instead of running toward His presence, Adam and Eve now dreaded the very presence of the One who loved them most. *Dread* is also known as an unhealthy fear that brings about anxiety.

Step 5: Death

By choosing to assert their will over God's will, Adam and Eve severed their relationship with God, leading to the exact consequence God warned Adam of—death. Ever since the fall, God has been unfolding the redemption plan He set out before He created the world: Jesus, the Lamb slain before the foundation of the world (Rev. 13:8). The Bible says about Jesus,

> ...who, being in very nature God, did not consider equality with God something to be used to his own advantage; rather, he made himself nothing by taking the very nature of a servant, being made in human likeness. And being found in appearance as a man, he humbled himself by becoming obedient to death—even death on a cross!
>
> —PHILIPPIANS 2:6–8

Jesus came to reverse the cycle of spiritual death passed down to us from our first parents, Adam and Eve. God sent Jesus to set free the captives entrapped by the enemy. Jesus came in humility, which is the kryptonite of narcissism. As we will go over in later chapters,

King Jesus chose to humble Himself and give Himself up for all of us so that by His victory we would have the chance to be reconciled to God. Satan doesn't want us to walk in that victory. His goal is to steal, kill, and destroy us (John 10:10).

To get his way either Satan will try to wreak havoc on your life to keep you from experiencing the freedom God purchased for you with His own blood, or he will deceive you with a false sense of security outside a relationship with Jesus. The Bible describes it this way: "In their case the god of this world [who is Satan] has blinded the minds of the unbelievers, to keep them from seeing the light of the gospel of the glory of Christ, who is the image of God" (2 Cor. 4:4, ESV).

I wanted to shed light on the original narcissist, Satan, because many people tend to limit the word *narcissist* to people without giving credit to the true source of narcissism—the devil. The Bible says, "For we do not wrestle against flesh and blood, but against the rulers, against the authorities, against the cosmic powers over this present darkness, against the spiritual forces of evil in the heavenly places" (Eph. 6:12, ESV). This includes the narcissistic individuals we are going to cover in upcoming chapters who are influenced by Satan's realm.

Defining Narcissism

Because of its increasing popularity, the term *narcissist* has unfortunately been used pretty loosely in recent years. This has led to many questions, including: What exactly is narcissism? How can I determine if someone in my life is a narcissist? What are the characteristics of a narcissist? Is there more than one type of narcissist? To answer these questions, it's important to understand the clinical criteria for diagnosing narcissistic personality disorder. But before we apply the criteria to those in our lives, let's first examine how Satan fits the criteria of a clinically narcissistic person.

So what exactly is narcissistic personality disorder (NPD)? Psychology looks at behavior to diagnose someone with a mental health disorder, and according to the *Diagnostic and Statistical Manual of Mental Disorders, Fifth Edition* (*DSM-5*)—the manual used by mental health professionals outlining symptoms that fit the criteria for particular mental health disorders—for a person to be diagnosed with narcissistic personality disorder, they must exhibit five of the nine characteristics of narcissism. As we look at the characteristics, you'll quickly see just how Satan meets not just the five needed to fit the bill but all of them, confirming that narcissism existed in him long before psychology discovered it.

Nine Telltale Signs of Narcissism

1. An inflated or exaggerated sense of self-importance

This first telltale sign of a narcissist is depicted in Isaiah 14:13–14 (NKJV), which recounts what led to Satan's fall:

> For you have said in your heart: "I will ascend into heaven, I will exalt my throne above the stars of God; I will also sit on the mount of the congregation on the farthest sides of the north; I will ascend above the heights of the clouds, I will be like the Most High."

2. An obsession with becoming the most

Whether that means becoming the most successful, the most powerful, the most beautiful, or the smartest person in the room, it is all to draw attention to the "self." It's no secret that Satan's quest to become *the most powerful* is what led him to fall from grace. The reference to Satan's aspiration to be "like the Most High" in Isaiah 14 doesn't insinuate Satan's desire to embody God's holy characteristics, such as His goodness, faithfulness, and love. This passage in Isaiah 14 makes it clear that what Satan was after was God's power. Satan's desire to exert power and control over the entire universe, including God Himself, shows just how exaggerated his sense of self-importance was and continues to be to this day.

This is a common trait of a narcissistic person that we will look into later in the book. In terms of beauty, theologians believe Satan was originally a magnificent angel. Unlike cartoon depictions, he was commonly referred to as an angel of light, referring to his beauty. Of him Ezekiel 28:13 says, "You were in Eden, the garden of God; every precious stone adorned you: carnelian, chrysolite and emerald, topaz, onyx and jasper, lapis lazuli, turquoise and beryl. Your settings and mountings were made of gold; on the day you were created they were prepared." Rather than praising his Creator for his beauty, however, Satan sought to bring attention and glory to himself instead of attributing glory to the only One who is worthy of it—God.

3. A belief they are special

They feel this way because of a position or status they hold. Before his fall, Satan held an honorable position in heaven, one that was given to him by God. Ezekiel 28:14 says, "You were anointed as a guardian cherub, for so I ordained you. You were on the holy mount of God; you walked among the fiery stones." At some point he stopped viewing his status as a gift from his Creator and started believing he *was* the gift.

4. A constant need for unwarranted admiration

Ezekiel 28:17 says of Satan, "Your heart became proud on account of your beauty, and you corrupted your wisdom because of your splendor." Satan, though created by God, wanted the Creator's position. He didn't deserve it. Yet his envy of God led him to plan to take over God's throne. Thousands of years later, at the cusp of Jesus' ministry, Matthew 4:8–9 says, "The devil took [Jesus] to a very high mountain and showed him all the kingdoms of the world and their splendor. 'All this I will give you,' he [Satan] said [to Jesus], 'if you will bow down and worship me.'"

In other words, the devil offered Jesus his version of "greatness" in exchange for Jesus' worship and adoration of him. To that, according to verse 10, Jesus said to him, "Away from me, Satan! For it is written: 'Worship the Lord your God, and serve him only.' In this scenario Satan, who is a created being, though aware of Jesus' divine identity, wanted Jesus to worship him. That, my friend, is the mindset of a narcissist.

5. A belief they are entitled to whatever they decide they want and going after it at any cost to others

Satan created a revolution in heaven in which he sought after God's glory, and in his quest he took down a third of heaven's angels with him (Rev. 12:4). The devil is an opportunist. He will keep watch, prowling (1 Pet. 5:8), looking for an opportunity to strike you down. Luke 4:13 recalls that when the devil finished tempting Jesus, he left him "until an opportune time."

6. Deception and exploitation of people to use for their advantage

A narcissistic person frequently resorts to manipulative behavior. They may even see people as a means to an end. Deception and exploitation are Satan's mode of operation from Genesis to Revelation.

7. A "hardened heart" and a lack of empathy for the person they're about to hurt

First Peter 5:8–9 offers the best explanation for this symptom: "Be alert and of sober mind. Your enemy the devil prowls around like a roaring lion looking for someone to devour. Resist him, standing firm in the faith, because you know that the family of believers throughout the world is undergoing the same kind of sufferings." Your enemy comes after you with everything he has. Thankfully, as this book will teach you, God has provided you with the resources to discern and exercise authority over deception and condemnation in any of the settings we will cover.

8. Resentment of anyone or anything that takes attention from them and a belief that people resent them because they are better

Satan couldn't stand that God was God and he was not, so he sought to take over His position. When he couldn't, he turned to Adam and Eve and now to you. As you'll see throughout this book, he uses a narcissist in your life to warp your sense of identity and induce chaos and confusion. As John 10:10 says, "The thief comes only to steal and kill and destroy."

9. A flaunting of their belief that they are better than those around them

In the midst of His ministry Jesus ran into some Jews who, much like Satan, were driven by pride. They put so much stock in their heritage that they looked past, and missed, God's redemption plan, who was standing before their very eyes. To this group Jesus said, "You belong to your father, the devil, and you want to carry out your father's desires. He was a murderer from the beginning, not holding to the truth, for there is no truth in him. When he lies, he speaks his native language, for he is a liar and the father of lies" (John 8:44).

Although Satan meets all nine traits, the reason a person needs to meet only five of the criteria rather than all nine is that the characteristics of narcissism listed represent two opposite personality traits. Some characterize a person who is loud by nature, while others describe someone who is quieter. In chapter 3 we will look at how Satan uses these two opposite personalities to his advantage to make two types of narcissists. Until then we're going to cover how someone becomes a narcissist.

Make It Personal

Seeing that it takes only five traits for someone to meet the criteria for narcissism, who throughout the course of your life has displayed five or more of those traits?

Name	Relation to you	How you were affected by their narcissism

Chapter 2

THE MAKING OF A NARCISSIST

As a counselor, I've come across so many individuals who have asked questions such as these:

» Are people born narcissistic, or is a narcissist made?

» How does someone become a narcissist?

» What are the contributing factors that lead to narcissism?

» Is narcissism curable?

» Can a child be narcissistic, or does narcissism affect only adults?

» Does having a narcissistic parent cause a child to become a narcissist?

Questions such as these are what this chapter aims to answer. As you read through these pages, my hope is that you will be able to follow the process by which a person becomes susceptible to narcissism.

As we've discussed so far, narcissism existed long before the diagnosis of NPD was established by mental health professionals. In chapter 1 we used Genesis 1–3 to explore how Satan employed a five-step destructive cycle to defeat Adam and Eve. At the point in which they acted in disobedience to God's command, they removed themselves from being submitted under Him and instead submitted themselves under the authority of the one they inclined their ears to—Satan. Their behavior after their disobedience is proof of that. Genesis recounts that once they disobeyed God, instead of running toward their Creator in humility, Adam and Eve attempted to hide their shame using external covering, marking the beginning of narcissism in mankind.

Just to be clear, I'm not calling everyone a narcissist. What I am making clear is that apart from Jesus, we all have the propensity toward narcissism. But we'll get to that later. For now let's continue with Adam and Eve. The Bible says,

> Then the man and his wife heard the sound of the Lord God as he was walking in the garden in the cool of the day, and they hid from the Lord God among the trees of the garden. But the Lord God called to the man, "Where are you?" He answered, "I heard you in the garden, and I

> was afraid because I was naked; so I hid." And he said, "Who told you that you were naked? Have you eaten from the tree that I commanded you not to eat from?" The man said, "The woman you put here with me—she gave me some fruit from the tree, and I ate it." Then the LORD God said to the woman, "What is this you have done?" The woman said, "The serpent deceived me, and I ate."
>
> —GENESIS 3:7–10

Adam and Eve's external covering proved insufficient to conceal them from their Creator. However, rather than admitting their faults and asking for mercy, they chose to shift the blame onto each other to save face with God. Unfortunately, they failed to realize that pride has no place in the presence of God.

Before Adam and Eve were driven out of the garden, God demonstrated His mercy and compassion by sacrificing a lamb and using its skin to clothe them, signifying the future sacrifice He would make on behalf of all mankind by sending Jesus, who was the Lamb slain from the foundations of the world. Ever since Adam and Eve's expulsion from the garden, marking their separation from God, God has been actively pursuing mankind to rescue us from our own self-destructive nature.

Narcissism, simply stated, is our willful alignment with our pride. By attempting to exert our will above God's will, which is intended for the ultimate good, we're essentially saying we are better, we know better, and we can do better.

Regarding the question "How does someone become a narcissist?" through much research scientists discovered two factors. The first is a *genetic predisposition to narcissism*. In 2014 the National Library of Medicine published a behavioral genetic study on narcissism finding that those who grow up to become narcissists have a gene that contributes to them becoming narcissists.[1] According to the *DSM-5*, although narcissism is more apparent in adolescence to early adulthood, narcissistic traits can be present in childhood.

These research findings confirm what the Bible says about mankind having a sinful nature at birth. David, the psalmist, said, "Surely I was sinful at birth, sinful from the time my mother conceived me" (Ps. 51:5). And the prophet Jeremiah said: "The heart is deceitful above all things and beyond cure. Who can understand it?" (Jer. 17:9).

After the fall, we all inherited the propensity toward narcissism. Our sinful nature, where we try to exert our will over God's will, drives us toward narcissism. The Bible explains our sinful nature this way:

> Those who live according to the flesh have their minds set on what the flesh desires; but those who live in accordance with the Spirit have their minds set on what the Spirit desires. The mind governed by the flesh is death, but the mind governed by the Spirit is life and peace. The mind governed by the flesh is hostile to God; it does not submit to

> God's law, nor can it do so. Those who are in the realm of the flesh cannot please God.
>
> —Romans 8:5–8

In the Old Testament, God gave the law to Moses to keep us within the guardrails of His will. Unfortunately, we don't have to read far into the Bible to see how people blatantly rejected God and behaved as they saw fit in their own eyes (Judg. 21:25), along with the consequences of their behavior. The Bible says it this way: "Pride goes before destruction, a haughty spirit before a fall" (Prov. 16:18).

The law didn't bring about transformation in people because of our natural resistance to living under God's authority, which only served as proof of how depraved the human heart truly is without God. In His perfect timing God sent His one and only Son to die for our sins, offering us the possibility to reconcile with Him by repenting—that is, turning away from our sinful nature and submitting to Jesus as our Lord and Savior. (See Romans 8:3 and John 3:16–17.)

So if God gave us the option of redemption, why does narcissism still exist? Narcissism is a matter of the heart. In Jesus, God gave us a choice to crucify the flesh and follow Him (Gal. 5:24). However, some of us choose to say, "I'm going to do what I want and how I see fit in my own eyes," instead.

Now, we all have moments when we mess up or blatantly do something to gratify our sinful nature. It goes to show that even as God's children we still have a sinful nature at work within us, but in Christ we have the freedom to choose whether to act on it. As Romans 8:9–14 (NLT) says,

> But you are not controlled by your sinful nature. You are controlled by the Spirit if you have the Spirit of God living in you. (And remember that those who do not have the Spirit of Christ living in them do not belong to him at all.) And Christ lives within you, so even though your body will die because of sin, the Spirit gives you life because you have been made right with God. The Spirit of God, who raised Jesus from the dead, lives in you. And just as God raised Christ Jesus from the dead, he will give life to your mortal bodies by this same Spirit living within you. Therefore, dear brothers and sisters, you have no obligation to do what your sinful nature urges you to do. For if you live by its dictates, you will die. But if through the power of the Spirit you put to death the deeds of your sinful nature, you will live. For all who are led by the Spirit of God are children of God.

While the first contributing factor in someone becoming a narcissist is *genetics*, the second is that person's *upbringing*. A study published by *BMC Psychiatry* (2024) found that narcissistic traits can develop from both parental overvaluation and living with unprocessed painful childhood experiences.[2] This means, according to this research, that either the narcissist in your life was raised as if they hung the moon—and they ran with it—or they experienced significant trauma that has gone unprocessed. Now they are displaying narcissistic traits as a defense mechanism to mask their deep-seated feelings of inadequacy.

To better illustrate the two contributing factors that can lead someone to becoming a narcissist, take a look at the following scenarios.

Arrested Development

Mary grew up in a household where her mother constantly overlooked and ignored her, which made her feel invisible and unimportant. Mary felt that her mother favored her brother more than her, and her father was rarely around because of his business trips. Mary grew up feeling insecure because her mom would often criticize her looks. Despite Mary's best efforts, she couldn't seem to meet the standards expected of her by her critical mother.

One day Mary made an inner vow that she would take care of herself and never look back. When she got older, Mary couldn't leave home fast enough. As soon as she was accepted at college, she packed her belongings and left. Mary's determination helped her accomplish the goals she had set for herself. She climbed the corporate ladder and swatted at anyone who got in her way.

Years into her career Mary got married and had children. As she was still operating out of an unhealed wound, Mary's job always took priority over her family's needs, as her job had been her escape for years. She didn't understand why her children were so needy. In fact, she couldn't stand the thought of babying them. Because Mary wasn't in touch with her emotions, she was unaware that the very thought of nurturing her children was a trigger that reminded her of how her mother once chose her brother over her. To avoid her trigger, Mary spent most of her time at work, where she was celebrated for her efforts.

Mary also had a temper. At home both her husband and her children learned quickly to read her cues to see if she was safe to approach or if today was going to be a bad day for them at home. Mary's children grew up to resent their mother for her lack of nurturing and resented their father for not standing up for them with their mom. According to Mary, however, she was a great mom. In fact, she felt that she did her children a favor by "getting them ready for the real world."

Mary's case is referred to as arrested development. This occurs when someone is raised in an environment that doesn't help develop their identity, combined with the fact that we're born with a sinful nature. Like with Mary, the person's emotional maturity becomes stagnant and resembles that of a toddler: "My way or the highway." Because it's learned behavior, through a relationship with Christ this person does have the potential to change, *if they choose to*. However, if they don't, and they choose not to deal with the hurt and resentment they've been burying for years, they become callous and in turn treat those around them as if they were objects to serve their needs.

Self-Inflated

Mary's brother, Simon, grew up as not only the baby of the family but also the favorite. In his mother's eyes Simon could do no wrong. Whatever Simon wanted, Simon got. Unlike his sister, who was treated harshly, Simon was treated as if he were the sun, and the world revolved around him. As he got older and began dating, Simon found it odd that his girlfriends didn't drop everything for him the way his mom did. So he resorted to shaming them and eventually breaking up with them.

Simon believed there was something inherently special about him, and when it was not recognized, he felt agitated and at times even offended. His confidence initially helped him land promotions. Unfortunately, he couldn't sustain a good team to work with him. Simon viewed his position as a leader no differently from his childhood—people were there for him, not the other way around.

At home his marriage was suffering. Simon's wife felt there was nothing she could do that would meet Simon's satisfaction. And he let her know it too. One day his wife decided to get herself and her children into counseling. Simon's wife worked with a Christian counselor, who helped her detach from the cycle of striving for Simon's approval and learn to attach her identity to the approval she already had in Jesus, a process we will delve into later in this book.

As Simon's wife began to see herself in Christ, Simon became more and more agitated. When he saw that she no longer viewed him as her everything, he decided to discard her by filing for a divorce. Simon and his wife went their separate ways.

Simon's case is referred to as the self-inflated narcissist. The issue with this narcissist is that they were highly praised for the very motives and actions God seeks to prune in us. Unfortunately, a person who became narcissistic through this route is much harder to change because they have deceived themselves that they are the god of their own lives and everyone else is here to serve their needs. Similar to Simon, people who depend on self-inflation have an ongoing desire for praise. When they don't receive the recognition or praise they expect, they feel cheated and lash out at the person they believe is withholding praise that belongs to them. The issue remains, however, that no amount of praise fills their grandiose appetite because they always want more.

As we've discussed in this chapter, we were all born with a sinful nature that has the propensity toward narcissism. However, God sent Jesus to set us free from the bondage of sin, and by the power of the Holy Spirit we are able to say no to our sinful nature and yes to God on a daily basis. The previous two scenarios also show how living with unhealed wounds or being raised with a sense of entitlement give Satan ground to foster and grow narcissism in your life.

I'm not saying that either upbringing will automatically cause one to become a narcissist. However, I've seen many cases where individuals chose not to heal from a traumatic childhood and instead harbored bitterness and entitlement, allowing Satan to gain a foothold in their life and lead it down a destructive path. I've also counseled and consulted on cases in which a person was raised in an environment where they were always the favorite, and Satan gained access into their lives by fueling their already inflated sense of pride. In this latter scenario Satan often doesn't have to do much to affirm the person that they are indeed special and can be their own god—and in turn reject their need for God.

As we've covered so far, two main factors contribute to someone becoming a narcissist: (1) genetics, in that we all inherited a sinful nature from our first parents, Adam and Eve; and (2) upbringing, whether the person was pampered, overvalued, or on the other extreme had endured painful experiences that turned into bitterness and entitlement. In either case choosing not to crucify our flesh but seeking our own will instead results in one of the two following ways someone becomes a narcissist:

Formula 1:
Sinful Nature + Self-Inflated = Narcissist

Formula 2:
Sinful Nature + Arrested Development = Narcissist

Make It Personal

Based on your knowledge of the individual(s) listed in chapter 1, write down their names and circle which scenario most likely led to their becoming a narcissist.

Name	Formula 1 or 2?
	Self-Inflated or Arrested Development
	Self-Inflated or Arrested Development
	Self-Inflated or Arrested Development
	Self-Inflated or Arrested Development
	Self-Inflated or Arrested Development
	Self-Inflated or Arrested Development
	Self-Inflated or Arrested Development
	Self-Inflated or Arrested Development
	Self-Inflated or Arrested Development
	Self-Inflated or Arrested Development

Because narcissists can be evasive at times, and may even fabricate stories about their lives, you may not know what their childhood entailed. The reason I asked this question is to help you track why the person acted the way they did—not to excuse their behavior but to help you see that there was nothing you could have done to fix it, an issue that many survivors of narcissistic abuse struggle with.

Chapter 3

TWO TYPES OF NARCISSISTS

THERE ARE TWO types of narcissists, both of which mirror Satan's characteristics that we covered in chapter 1. The first type of narcissist is the *power-hungry narcissist.* Infamous for their arrogance, ruthlessness, and need for control, this type of narcissist creates fear in their environment to try to subdue those around them. To give you a better understanding of this type of narcissist, let's look at the two Bible characters who embody it.

POWER-HUNGRY NARCISSISTS

Pharaoh of Egypt

The first is Pharaoh. Exodus describes Pharaoh as a king who used his role to control and oppress those under him. Like a true narcissist, Pharaoh viewed people as tools to be used at his disposal. A narcissist is driven by a deep-seated fear of losing control. Exodus 1:9–11 recalls how after Pharaoh came into power, he said,

> "Look…the Israelites have become far too numerous for us. Come, we must deal shrewdly with them or they will become even more numerous and, if war breaks out, will join our enemies, fight against us and leave the country." So they put slave masters over them to oppress them with forced labor, and they built Pithom and Rameses as store cities for Pharaoh.

A power-hungry narcissist uses fear to force people into submission, leaving those in his circle feeling as if they have no choice but to comply with him as a means of survival because oftentimes the victim's exit comes at a great cost.

Similar to his role model, the devil, a narcissist considers himself a god to those around him and will likely dismiss anyone who questions his inflated self-image, particularly when it involves surrendering to God. When the Lord called Moses to free the Israelites, God told Moses to go to Pharaoh and tell him, "This is what the Lord, the God of Israel, says: 'Let my people go, so that they may hold a festival to me in the wilderness.' Pharaoh said, 'Who is the Lord, that I should obey him and let Israel go? I do not know the Lord and I will not let Israel go'" (Exod. 5:1–2).

When Pharaoh felt challenged, the Bible says in verses 6–19,

> That same day Pharaoh gave this order to the slave drivers and overseers in charge of the people: "You are no longer to supply the people with straw for making bricks; let them go and gather their own straw. But require them to make the same number of bricks as before; don't reduce the quota. They are lazy; that is why they are crying out, 'Let us go and sacrifice to our God.' Make the work harder for the people so that they keep working and pay no attention to lies."
>
> Then the slave drivers and the overseers went out and said to the people, "This is what Pharaoh says: 'I will not give you any more straw. Go and get your own straw wherever you can find it, but your work will not be reduced at all.'" So the people scattered all over Egypt to gather stubble to use for straw. The slave drivers kept pressing them, saying, "Complete the work required of you for each day, just as when you had straw." And Pharaoh's slave drivers beat the Israelite overseers they had appointed, demanding, "Why haven't you met your quota of bricks yesterday or today, as before?"
>
> Then the Israelite overseers went and appealed to Pharaoh: "Why have you treated your servants this way? Your servants are given no straw, yet we are told, 'Make bricks!' Your servants are being beaten, but the fault is with your own people."
>
> Pharaoh said, "Lazy, that's what you are—lazy! That is why you keep saying, 'Let us go and

> sacrifice to the Lord.' Now get to work. You will not be given any straw, yet you must produce your full quota of bricks."
>
> The Israelite overseers realized they were in trouble when they were told, "You are not to reduce the number of bricks required of you for each day." When they left Pharaoh, they found Moses and Aaron waiting to meet them, and they said, "May the Lord look on you and judge you! You have made us obnoxious to Pharaoh and his officials and have put a sword in their hand to kill us."

As you see from this account, the power-hungry narcissist will seek to divide and conquer. Pharaoh oppressed those under him to the point where they couldn't bear it, and out of fear those who were oppressed turned against the very person God was using to liberate them.

In the same way, the narcissist in your life uses fear to oppress you. A power-hungry narcissist believes you are *theirs*—whether that's their possession, their protégé, their property. In their mind, they own you. They see you as inferior to themselves and sees your existence as merely for their benefit. As you'll see from the coming chapters, this narcissist banks on the fact that you don't have a true sense of self. So they sweep right in to feed your already existing fear of being alone in the world, or that you'll never measure up, or that something is wrong with you. That is, if they didn't contribute to you developing a fractured view of identity to begin with, as in the cases of a narcissistic parent.

Like their puppet master, Satan, a power-hungry

narcissist can smell weakness from a mile away. Their weapon of choice is fear, and they use it as their right of passage to shake you at your core. In their mind if you fall for their fear tactics, you'll be shaken up, which will ultimately lead you to turn to them, your abuser, for help, putting you right back into his cycle.

That's what Pharaoh did to the Israelites. The closer they were to obtaining their deliverance, the worse he treated them. Even when Pharaoh saw the finger of God at work, over and over, he refused to comply with God because in his heart he too was a "god," much like how his true father, the devil, felt in his own heart. Even when Pharaoh finally let the Israelites go, because it was not an act done out of true obedience and a change of heart, he chased after his perceived possessions unto his death. As you see through the historical accounts of the Israelites, even after God had delivered them from the hands of their narcissist, they were still bound by the spirit of bondage, traps we will deal with in part 2 of the book.

Queen Jezebel

Another power-hungry narcissist Scripture highlights is Jezebel, the wife of King Ahab. During her reign as queen, Jezebel pushed Baal worship across the nation of Israel, the same nation that God had delivered out of the hands of Pharaoh years prior. Jezebel was so determined to convert these Israelites that she went after God's prophets, killed them, and replaced them with her own false prophets. When the prophet Elijah challenged the credibility of Jezebel's prophets, proved they were fake, and killed them, the Bible says,

> So Jezebel sent a messenger to Elijah to say, "May the gods deal with me, be it ever so severely, if by this time tomorrow I do not make your life like that of one of them." Elijah was afraid and ran for his life. When he came to Beersheba in Judah, he left his servant there, while he himself went a day's journey into the wilderness. He came to a broom bush, sat down under it and prayed that he might die. "I have had enough, Lord," he said. "Take my life; I am no better than my ancestors."
>
> —1 Kings 19:1–4

This, my friend, is how a power-hungry narcissist makes you feel. They entice fear even in those who try to lead God-honoring lives. At times it may even seem like the closer you walk with God, the worse that narcissist in your life treats you. The reason I wanted to include this part is to bring you back to the reality that your fight is truly against the spiritual forces at work in that person's life, something we will cover more in detail throughout the book.

Undercover Narcissists

The second type of narcissist is the *undercover narcissist.* Unlike the first type, who leads with fear and projects arrogance, this one projects a ton of charm, but underneath the veil of charm is a yawning chasm of deceit, prowling and calculating the next move that will ensure their goals are met, at whatever cost. This narcissist will prioritize their interests above relationships. They exploit and manipulate others to get ahead in life. And much like their role model, the devil, they will lie and deceive and even destroy as they see fit to get where and what they want.

Unlike the power-hungry narcissist, who flaunts their power in arrogance, the undercover narcissist is much harder to pinpoint because they lie beneath the surface, scheming and watching for an opportune time to take their prey captive, just as the devil does.

Delilah

Delilah is a great example of an undercover narcissist. The Book of Judges tells the story of Samson, a man God had appointed before he was even born to defeat the Philistines. Before his birth, the angel of the Lord appeared to Samson's mom with orders from heaven to consecrate Samson to the Lord's service and to follow certain ordinances God had put in place for him. The Bible says Samson's parents followed what God commanded them in raising Samson, and when he grew, God's Spirit was manifested in him through supernatural strength.

But from his young adulthood Samson had a weakness—something we will dive into more in part 2 of the book. The enemy used Samson's weakness for women as a way to try to defeat him.

> [Samson] fell in love with a woman in the Valley of Sorek whose name was Delilah. The rulers of the Philistines went to her and said, "See if you can lure him into showing you the secret of his great strength and how we can overpower him so we may tie him up and subdue him. Each one of us will give you eleven hundred shekels of silver." So Delilah said to Samson, "Tell me the secret of your great strength and how you can be tied up and subdued." Samson answered her, "If anyone ties me with seven fresh bowstrings that have not been dried, I'll become as weak as any other man." Then the rulers of the Philistines brought her seven fresh bowstrings that had not been dried, and she tied him with them. With men hidden in the room, she called to him, "Samson, the Philistines are upon you!" But he snapped the bowstrings as easily as a piece of string snaps when it comes close to a flame. So the secret of his strength was not discovered.
>
> —Judges 16:4–9

We would think that at this point Samson would see through Delilah's deception, but he didn't. Delilah continued to charm him and even went so far as to manipulate him into having to prove to her that he truly loved her. "Delilah said to him, "How can you say, 'I love you,' when you won't confide in me? This is the third time you have made a fool of me and haven't told me the secret of your great strength" (v. 15). See how she twisted the situation to play the victim and manipulate him into revealing his secret? The story continues, "With such nagging she prodded him day after day until he was sick to death of it" (v. 16). Let's keep reading.

> So he told her everything. "No razor has ever been used on my head," he said, "because I have been a Nazirite dedicated to God from my mother's womb. If my head were shaved, my strength would leave me, and I would become as weak as any other man."
>
> When Delilah saw that he had told her everything, she sent word to the rulers of the Philistines, "Come back once more; he has told me everything." So the rulers of the Philistines returned with the silver in their hands. After putting him to sleep on her lap, she called for someone to shave off the seven braids of his hair, and so began to subdue him. And his strength left him. Then she called, "Samson, the Philistines are upon you!"
>
> He awoke from his sleep and thought, "I'll go out as before and shake myself free." But he did not know that the LORD had left him. Then the Philistines seized him, gouged out his eyes and took him down to Gaza. Binding him with bronze shackles, they set him to grinding grain in the prison.
>
> —JUDGES 16:16–21

Delilah's exploitation of Samson's vulnerability shows not only a lack of empathy on her part but also just how far she was willing to go in pursuit of her ultimate goal, regardless of whom she hurt in the long run.

Jacob

A second example of an undercover narcissist is one whose name in Hebrew means "he grasps the heel," a Hebrew idiom for *he takes advantage of* or *he deceives.* That is, Jacob. As we discussed earlier, an undercover narcissist uses lies and deception and may even resort to exploiting people to get ahead, regardless of the consequences to those he exploits. Jacob was the second-born of twins, which meant his brother, Esau, was the rightful recipient of the firstborn right, giving him a double portion of his father's inheritance.

One of the characteristics of an undercover narcissist, as we've seen, is that he exploits a person's weakness and uses it to his advantage. In Jacob's case Genesis 25:29–33 recalls:

> Once when Jacob was cooking some stew, Esau came in from the open country, famished. He said to Jacob, "Quick, let me have some of that red stew! I'm famished!" (That is why he was also called Edom.) Jacob replied, "First sell me your birthright." "Look, I am about to die," Esau said. "What good is the birthright to me?" But Jacob said, "Swear to me first." So he swore an oath to him, selling his birthright to Jacob.

Genesis 27:1–12 continues the account:

> When Isaac was old and his eyes were so weak that he could no longer see, he called for Esau his older son and said to him, "My son." "Here I am,"

> he answered. Isaac said, "I am now an old man and don't know the day of my death. Now then, get your equipment—your quiver and bow—and go out to the open country to hunt some wild game for me. Prepare me the kind of tasty food I like and bring it to me to eat, so that I may give you my blessing before I die."
>
> Now Rebekah was listening as Isaac spoke to his son Esau. When Esau left for the open country to hunt game and bring it back, Rebekah said to her son Jacob, "Look, I overheard your father say to your brother Esau, 'Bring me some game and prepare me some tasty food to eat, so that I may give you my blessing in the presence of the LORD before I die.' Now, my son, listen carefully and do what I tell you: Go out to the flock and bring me two choice young goats, so I can prepare some tasty food for your father, just the way he likes it. Then take it to your father to eat, so that he may give you his blessing before he dies."
>
> Jacob said to Rebekah his mother, "But my brother Esau is a hairy man while I have smooth skin. What if my father touches me? I would appear to be tricking him and would bring down a curse on myself rather than a blessing."

Note here that Jacob didn't refuse his mom's deceptive request out of love for his brother or the fact that he would be lying to his dad. He refused it out of fear that the plan may not work and otherwise backfire on him, bringing a curse down on his life. But when "His mother said to him, 'My son, let the curse fall on me. Just do what I say; go and get them for me'" (v. 13), Jacob moved forward with the plan to deceive his dad and steal his brother's birthright.

After disguising himself with the help of his mother, Jacob "went to his father and said, 'My father.' 'Yes, my son,' he answered. 'Who is it?' Jacob said to his father, 'I am Esau your firstborn. I have done as you told me. Please sit up and eat some of my game, so that you may give me your blessing'" (vv. 18–19).

An undercover narcissist will lie and literally not feel bad about it. Isaac asked his son, "'How did you find it so quickly, my son?' 'The LORD your God gave me success,' he replied" (v. 20). Jacob knew his father worshipped the LORD, and so he used that to his advantage to insinuate that God gave him success. Another way an undercover narcissist manipulates those he targets: He pays attention to what's important to them, as we will see in the coming chapters, and uses that as the framework of his attack.

The account continues:

> Then Isaac said to Jacob, "Come near so I can touch you, my son, to know whether you really are my son Esau or not." Jacob went close to his father Isaac, who touched him and said, "The voice is the voice of Jacob, but the hands are the hands of Esau." He did not recognize him, for his hands were hairy like those of his brother Esau; so

> he proceeded to bless him. "Are you really my son Esau?" he asked. "I am," he replied.
>
> —Genesis 27:21–24

Another lie. As you may already know, this deceptive trick worked and led to Jacob receiving the blessing of the firstborn. When Esau found out that Jacob stole his blessing, he chased after Jacob, and Jacob fled to his uncle Laban's home—where he discovered through the ensuing years that his uncle was his match in undercover narcissism. While living with Laban, Jacob fell in love with Rachel and agreed to work for her father for seven years in exchange for her hand in marriage. Laban, recognizing God's favor on Jacob, took advantage of him and deceived him into marrying Leah instead of Rachel, leading Jacob to work for an additional seven years to marry Rachel.

Although Jacob fit the bill for a con artist—and someone unlikely to ever overcome his narcissistic nature—he bears evidence that no type of narcissist is beyond God's reach. Eventually God changed Jacob's name to Israel, or "one who prevails with God," and he became a father of the faith.

To summarize, and to give you a visual of the main differences between a power-hungry narcissist and an undercover narcissist, take a look at the following chart:

The Power-Hungry Narcissist	The Undercover Narcissist
Loud	Quiet
Uses fear to control	Uses guilt to manipulate
Openly self-centered	Seeks attention through victimhood or pity
Impulsive	Calculated
Cruel	Secretive
Aggressive	Passive-aggressive

The factors that influence whether someone is a power-hungry narcissist versus an undercover narcissist depend on the person's God-given traits, which the enemy in turn uses for his evil purposes.

MAKE IT PERSONAL

Using the list of narcissists you've dealt with in your life, write down each name and circle the type of narcissist they are.

Name	Type
	Power-Hungry or Undercover
	Power-Hungry or Undercover
	Power-Hungry or Undercover
	Power-Hungry or Undercover
	Power-Hungry or Undercover
	Power-Hungry or Undercover
	Power-Hungry or Undercover
	Power-Hungry or Undercover
	Power-Hungry or Undercover

Chapter 4

THREE WAYS NARCISSISTS SHOW UP IN YOUR LIFE

NARCISSISTS CAN ASSUME different roles in your life. Depending on the stage of life you're in, your enemy entices people—whether they know it or not—to do his bidding. The reason I say this is that there are narcissistic people who blatantly try to hurt you, while others are merely exploited by the enemy to use their unhealed wounds to inflict or project their pain onto you. The narcissistic people your enemy uses typically fall into three categories. It's important to keep in mind that some people may fit into multiple categories, causing their impact on your life to overlap.

The Narcissistic Authority Figure

An authority figure is someone who has accepted the responsibility to steward and care for the well-being of the person in their care for a certain amount of time. A narcissistic authority figure, however, is someone who flips the script to "It is the person's responsibility to look after my well-being whether by making me look good or by serving as my tool for emotional support."

People who fall under the umbrella of authority figures include parents, stepparents, grandparents, caregivers, bosses, mentors, or pastors, among others. In other words, the authority figure includes anyone in a position of authority over you. Narcissistic authority figures see themselves as the main characters in your life, while you exist to be their supportive role, even if it's to your detriment.

As a trauma counselor, I'd say one of the most painful and difficult cases to treat is the person who has been abused by a narcissistic authority figure. If you've experienced abuse by a narcissistic authority figure, I'm sure you've wondered why and how Satan enticed that person specifically to hurt you. Here's the answer: Satan knows the amount of influence authority figures have on people. Whether that person is your parent or they hold a mentor role in your life, Satan knows that a narcissistic authority figure makes for the perfect instrument to exploit a person when they are in a vulnerable stage of their life.

From a physical perspective, this includes cases of physical or sexual abuse. From an emotional perspective, it includes cases in which the authority figure speaks hurtful words over the person in their care. From a spiritual perspective, it includes cases where the authority figure exploits the person when they are spiritually vulnerable. Having studied humanity for centuries, the devil knows that authority figures significantly shape a person's self-image, worldview, and, above all, connection with God.

The Narcissistic Peer

Unlike authority figures, peers are those we relate to from an equal, or level, playing field. A peer can be a sibling or another family member who is around the same age as you, a spouse or romantic partner, a friend, a classmate, a coworker, a business partner, and so forth.

The reason the enemy likes to use a narcissist in the role of a peer is that you're more likely to let your guard down with a peer. The fear of judgment drops drastically with someone you perceive as being on an equal playing field.

So how does the enemy like to use this person? He will often insert someone in your life to get you to stray little by little from doing what is right ("bad company corrupts good character," 1 Cor. 15:33), or he may employ more drastic measures by placing someone in your life who is a constant source of heartache or headache.

Over the years, I've treated many siblings of narcissists

who carried so many wounds as a result of the way their siblings treated them growing up. I've also treated patients whose source of daily heartache was a narcissistic coworker with a vendetta against them. The enemy loves throwing darts at you through them in the hopes that their darts will pierce past your thoughts and take root in your heart. When that happens, if the darts are not uprooted, Satan can get a foothold in your life (Eph. 4:29). We will cover this process in part 2.

The Narcissistic Protégé

While we may look up to an authority figure and do life with someone in a peer role, a protégé is often someone we invest our time and resources in, and we may even sacrifice from our life to help them in some way. People who fall under the umbrella of protégés may be siblings who are much younger, our children, grandchildren, mentees, interns, employees under our leadership, disciples, and so forth. Anyone who looks up to you and whose life you're investing in would fall into the category of a protégé.

Sometimes the enemy will use a narcissistic protégé in your life based on an unhealed wound you have. For example, let's say you've been through an abusive situation that you haven't healed from. You've just kept going with your life. One day you meet someone who's going through a similar situation to what you went through years ago. Moved by the person's situation, you jump at the thought of helping that person get out of it. Weeks (or months) later you find yourself so involved in this person's life, trying to rescue them from their situation, that some of your priorities are taking the back seat.

At times you may even notice that the person you're helping isn't as motivated as you are to get them out of the situation. Or you take on too much responsibility for them and become overwhelmed by it all. Or you might notice that they're ungrateful or even expect the help you're offering.

You may ask yourself, "How in the world did I get here?" Well, the enemy knows that unhealed wounds block your ability to exercise logic in areas the wound is associated with.

That's why it's so important that you ask the Lord if an opportunity to help someone is from Him or if Satan is exploiting an unhealed wound in your life. Do not make a hasty decision based on emotion. Another tactic the enemy will use is to infiltrate your life with a protégé who admires you. It's so important to watch out for this tactic, especially if you didn't receive praise growing up, or if your current home life is devoid of encouragement. Falling for or even entertaining ego strokes can lead to a downward spiral.

Now, there are times in which you mentor a protégé from the heart and that person displays neither of the two characteristics we just discussed. That is until one day they betray you, and you're left feeling confused and hurt, trying to piece together the scenarios and conversations to figure out where everything went wrong. That's when the enemy comes in to plant bitterness, anger, and resentment in your heart so he can take hold of you.

Satan loves hurting people, whether by using a narcissistic authority figure, luring someone in the role of a peer, or enticing a protégé you've invested in to turn around and betray you. Because we live in a fallen, broken world and carry within us our flesh, barring God's healing, narcissistic abuse lands us in one of four traps, all of which characterize bondage in some shape or form. In the next chapter we will dive into the four traps of narcissistic abuse.

Make It Personal

Now that you understand the various roles a narcissistic person can have in your life and how each role can impact you differently, let's see if Satan has tried to exploit your life using people in specific roles more than others. To identify any pattern in the roles Satan uses, write down each name from your list of narcissists once again and circle the role(s) they have had in your life. Take note of any patterns in the roles Satan often exploits—for instance, a pattern of dating one narcissist after another. Or of falling victim to narcissistic abuse by authority figures, beginning from childhood by a parent, through adulthood by a boss, and so forth. I've noticed in my life and in my patients' lives that Satan will often use people in one particular role over the rest.

Name	Role
	Authority — Peer — Protégé
	Authority — Peer — Protégé
	Authority — Peer — Protégé
	Authority — Peer — Protégé
	Authority — Peer — Protégé
	Authority — Peer — Protégé
	Authority — Peer — Protégé
	Authority — Peer — Protégé
	Authority — Peer — Protégé
	Authority — Peer — Protégé

Chapter 5

FOUR TRAPS OF NARCISSISTIC ABUSE

Genesis 3:7 recalls that when Adam and Eve fell for the original narcissist's schemes, rather than crying out to their Father, "they sewed fig leaves together and made coverings for themselves." Like Adam and Eve, when we fall prey to narcissistic abuse, our first inclination is to try to fix the situation on our own—usually in a way we believe will shield us from feeling exposed. The problem with this approach is that it lands us in one of the four traps the enemy set out for us to begin with.

These traps are mindsets that prevent us from living in the freedom God has given us through Jesus. Imagine each trap as a deep hole dug by the enemy that he hid under a layer of leaves. The enemy uses narcissistic people to sway you from God's direction for your life to try to get you to fall into one of his hidden traps. The issue with these traps is that we can get stuck in them for so long we start to identify ourselves by them.

Throughout this chapter we're going to explore four stories, each representing one of the four traps we fall into due to narcissistic abuse. As you read these stories, you may find that one or more of these mindsets resonates with you.

The Trap of Self-Defeat

Lana, a thirty-six-year-old patient, came into the office for an assessment following her discharge from an inpatient facility for attempting to take her own life. After going through her family history, it was clear to me that Lana was stuck in a self-inflicted destructive cycle. Her chart was packed with disorders for which she met the clinical criteria—disorders that had become labels she wore in addition to the ones put on her growing up. During her childhood and teenage years, Lana's dad served in the military. His absence created added stress on her mom. Lana described her mom as very critical of her and said her mother often told her that she reminded her of her father, "and not in a good way."

Lana and her mother didn't have much in common. For example, Lana described herself as a "feeler," in contrast to her mom, whom she described as more of a "thinker." Throughout the years, Lana tried her best to get her mom's approval, but it seemed that every time she tried, her mother would raise the bar higher, eventually convincing Lana that she could never measure up. When Lana was five, her mom gave birth to a baby boy. Initially Lana was so happy to have a baby brother. However, at around age eight, Lana began to feel resentment toward her baby brother because it seemed as though her mom loved him more, paid attention to him more, and cared for him more.

As a teenager, when Lana developed the courage to share her feelings with her mother, she responded with, "Why are you so jealous?" and, "You're just being dramatic," along with other statements insinuating that Lana's feelings were mere figments of her imagination. As the years went on, her mom's favoritism toward her brother was even more apparent. As a coping mechanism, Lana resorted to denying her need for her mother's love and met that need through self-destructive measures. She cut herself to numb her pain. She tried wearing crystals to manifest good energy in herself. She tried drinking, partying, anything to fill the void she had deep within her heart, to no avail.

As she became older, Lana found herself attracted to men who treated her the same way her mom did. Her relationships, one after another, wouldn't last because it seemed as though each man she was romantically involved with refused to prioritize her. The one time Lana met someone who treated her with kindness and gentleness, Lana pushed him away because the way he treated her didn't match her ingrained beliefs about herself—that she was unworthy, unlovable.

During her time at the mental health facility, Lana gave her life to Jesus, yet she continued to experience symptoms of anxiety and depression. "If this Jesus is supposed to give me freedom, why do I always feel tormented? Why won't He stop my panic attacks? Why won't He help me?" she cried out as tears rolled down her cheeks.

Lana's life was marked by a trap she had fallen into from narcissistic abuse—in this case, by an authority figure, her mother. Even as an adult, Lana continued to believe the words once spoken over her by her narcissistic parent, giving the enemy a foothold to induce more destructive thoughts and leading her to a life of chaos.

Filled with shame and convinced she could never amount to anything, Lana alternated between denying her need for love and seeking out love using unhealthy measures. Even in instances when someone tried to love her, because that person's behavior didn't match how she felt about herself, Lana pushed them away.

Stuck in a continuous cycle of self-defeat, Lana's life was marked by chaos, unstable relationships, and mood swings. She sabotaged good opportunities that came her way because she felt unworthy of them. Throughout counseling, Lana narrowed down her thought process to "If my mom/dad didn't love me, then I must be unlovable. And because I am unlovable, when people get close to me, they will leave me."

Throughout the months that followed her first session, Lana and I worked through the process we will go over later in the book. Within a few months Lana's depression dissipated, her anxiety was gone, and her panic attacks diminished by 90 percent. I say 90 percent because the devil always looks for opportune times to come after us, but when Lana feels an attack coming on, she now knows how to take authority over it—something I will teach you later in this book.

The Trap of Rebellion

Katrina, a forty-seven-year-old patient, came into the office with symptoms of dysthymia, another word for stubborn depression that just won't go away. This type of depression comes from feeling unsatisfied with life. She also experienced panic attacks that would come on all of a sudden. Katrina was a successful attorney, married, with four children. On the outside her life reflected many people's dream lives, but behind closed doors it was imploding.

Growing up in a home where her father constantly put her and her mother down, Katrina made a vow to herself early on that she would never let a man treat her the way her dad treated her. And that vow, she held to. Katrina worked hard to put herself through law school. Years later she married and started a family. Throughout her marriage and parenting, Katrina and her husband struggled with Katrina's constant need to control, not allowing her husband to lead the home. Katrina also struggled with undermining what her husband said to their children. As a result, he would often feel disrespected and shut down. That caused Katrina's anxiety to skyrocket and eventually led her to mimic her dad's behaviors—the very behaviors she grew up hating about her father.

Katrina was stuck repeating a cycle she had run from for so long, causing her to despise herself. Her problem was that she longed for intimacy, but the wound from her father was still very much alive. It created anxiety related to intimacy with the very person she'd said, "I do," to. In fact, Katrina would often treat her husband with the same loathing she carried in her heart toward her father. And she didn't know how to stop it.

Meanwhile, at work Katrina caught the attention of her coworker Ross. Gregarious and charming, Ross would consistently compliment Katrina's work, acknowledging her skills and dedication. At times Ross even went beyond professional compliments, commenting on her personality and looks. Katrina felt flattered by the attention. "At least someone appreciates me around here," the enemy whispered in her mind, using her voice. "Look at Ross. He's not intimidated by a strong, determined woman like me. That's because he has it together, unlike the loser I have at home, who can't even seem to cut the grass when I ask him to!"

One day after Katrina and her husband argued about him forgetting to run an errand she had asked him to do for the thousandth time, the enemy whispered, "Look at the way Ross carries himself. That's the type of man I deserve. And out of all the staff, he sees me!"

As time went on, Ross' compliments became more frequent and personal. He started inviting Katrina to after-work events and lunches, often finding ways to be alone with her. Deep down, Katrina knew something was wrong. But she struggled with denying her need to be loved when someone was offering the very thing she yearned for.

You see how the enemy entered Katrina's life? Her unresolved resentment toward her father caused her to guard herself against the person she was "one" with. Her need to feel loved, however, didn't go away, so the enemy presented an alternative, a less threatening alternative: Ross. Her brain didn't associate him with a perceived threat in the same way it connected her husband to her father.

Katrina's hunger for an emotional connection made her vulnerable to the enemy's attack. The compliments she received, especially from someone she esteemed as important, felt good. Katrina gave in to Ross' flattery. Her interactions with him soon turned into him asking her to accompany him on a business trip. Katrina knew the temptation she was putting herself in, but rather than escaping out of temptation (1 Cor. 10:13), she fell right into the trap the enemy had set out for her. "After all, it's just a business trip," the enemy whispered in her mind.

A few business trips later, Katrina had inappropriate encounters with Ross, who by the way was also married and had no intention of leaving his wife. You see, Ross viewed Katrina as someone who was there to entertain him. A narcissistic peer, like Satan, doesn't have a conscience. He sees those in relation to him as able bodies to be used at his disposal. When Katrina met with Ross to talk to him about how guilty she felt, Ross denied responsibility and reminded Katrina that she was an adult who knew what she was getting into. He told her it was not his responsibility to babysit her emotions—reflecting his master, Satan's behavior. He will tempt you over and over until you fall, and when you do, he will accuse you and condemn you for the very thing he tempted you to do.

As part of God's protective love toward us, He convicts us when we act in a way that contradicts who we are in Him. As a result of her inappropriate encounters, Katrina felt tormented for weeks. During those times, the enemy whispered in her mind, "Don't tell your husband now; what's done is done," to try to keep her bound. Then when she kept silent, he whispered, "How can you call yourself a Christian and do what you did?"—accusing her of the very thing he tempted her to do. At night he'd whisper, "What is everyone going to think of you when this comes out?"—using her weakness, fear of ridicule, against her so she would stay bound in her sin.

After his affair with Bathsheba, King David said,

> When I kept silent, my bones wasted away through my groaning all day long. For day and night your hand was heavy on me; my strength was sapped as in the heat of summer. Then I acknowledged my sin to you and did not cover up my iniquity. I said, "I will confess my transgressions to the Lord." And you forgave the guilt of my sin.
>
> —Psalm 32:3–5

Like David, Katrina understood that when you belong to God, He will not let you rest in keeping your sin a secret, because God knows that unexposed sin gives a foothold to the enemy of your soul. To eradicate sin, you have to expose it so you can begin healing, which includes understanding what led you down that path to begin with.

After countless sleepless nights, Katrina finally came clean to her husband. She and her husband worked on their marriage with the help of a Christian counselor. Meanwhile Katrina completed the steps outlined in part 2 of this book to heal past wounds the enemy was using against them in their marriage.

The Trap of Over-Accommodating

Elizabeth, a fifty-eight-year-old patient, came into counseling because of ongoing panic attacks she had struggled with off and on for years. She had been married for thirty-four years, and recently she and her husband had been arguing over the fact that she constantly dropped everything for her daughter. Whenever I treat someone, regardless of their age, I like to explore their history from as early as they can remember, and as the patient recalls their story, I pray for discernment and a word of knowledge.

In Elizabeth's case, she was raised in a loving home. Her parents provided her with a steady upbringing. The only thing that stood out was that she lost her mother not long after she and her husband were married. Elizabeth mentioned that she was so excited to become a parent.

In raising her daughter, determined to be the best mom she could be, Elizabeth often gave in to her daughter's requests, basking in the excitement of being a mother. From early motherhood Elizabeth got in the habit of giving in to most of her daughter's requests, chalking it up to, "You have to choose your battles," and, "They're only little once!"

As Elizabeth's daughter became older, she never seemed to get the hang of adult responsibility. She'd often call her mom, who would come to her rescue. This pattern created financial hardship in Elizabeth and her husband's life. Elizabeth would often tell her husband, "Well, you never stop being a mom," to excuse herself, dropping everything to help her reckless daughter. Whenever Elizabeth did stand up to her daughter, her daughter would excommunicate her, causing Elizabeth to become depressed and eventually give in. It wasn't until Elizabeth began to cash in her retirement to help her daughter that she sought counseling.

Through counseling Elizabeth was able to make the connection that around the time when she had her daughter, she also lost her mother. Her life was so busy she never grieved the loss of her mother, and instead she turned to her daughter for comfort to fill that void and to keep herself from feeling the turmoil within. She focused on becoming the best mom she could be for her daughter. Elizabeth was able to realize that the anxiety she felt from her daughter's threats to withdraw her love was due to the fact that her daughter had become her source of comfort since her mom's passing. Elizabeth went through the steps to heal from narcissistic abuse, as outlined in part 2. Within months she was able to set boundaries with her daughter, heal her marriage, and reclaim her freedom.

The Trap of Arrogance

I wish I could tell you that twenty-six-year-old Lilly was a patient. Unfortunately, a person who fits this characteristic doesn't seek counseling because they've convinced themselves that everyone else is the problem. Lilly was raised by an emotionally healthy father and a mother who over-accommodated her. On a side note, a narcissist and a person stuck in the trap of over-accommodating often have a way of finding each other, whether in a romantic relationship or, as in this case, a parent-child relationship. This is because the narcissist's motto is "You're here to meet my needs," while the over-accommodating party's motto is "I'm here to meet your needs."

From a young age, Lilly learned how to get her mom to do what she wanted her to do. She wasn't a fan of her dad, however, because he saw right through her. Enticed by Satan, the author of chaos, Lilly would often pit her mom against her dad, resulting in arguments and friction in the home. Lilly would also alternate between using charm and guilt-trip methods, knowing her mom would oblige her requests.

As Lilly got older, she became more dissatisfied with how the world operated. She felt that her teachers and, later on, her employers needed to project the same understanding her mom did growing up. As a result, Lilly couldn't keep a job, which led her to rely on her mom to help her. Lilly's love life was marked by a series of failed relationships, one after another. Lilly felt that her boyfriends were supposed to compliment her, acknowledge her, encourage her, and be a constant reminder of how special she was. When they failed to do so, she felt angry and offended and displayed emotionally explosive outbursts—followed by breaking up with them and looking for (and finding) someone who did.

One day when Lilly's mom finally stood her ground, Lilly was taken aback at her mother's audacity to say no to her. After all, she seldom said no growing up. Lilly blamed her father for her mom's boundaries. And when her attempts to turn them against one another failed, she excommunicated her mom until she needed her again.

Make It Personal

Which of the previous stories or situations do you resonate with?

PART II
OVERCOMING NARCISSISTIC ABUSE

Chapter 6

"WHERE ARE YOU?"

IN THE PREVIOUS chapter we went over how Adam and Eve tried to cover themselves up. After they did, the Bible recalls, "The man and his wife heard the sound of the Lord God as he was walking in the garden in the cool of the day, and they hid from the LORD God among the trees of the garden" (Gen. 3:8). Then God asked Adam, "Where are you?"

This question was meant to induce self-reflection. We'll never know what would've happened had Adam and Eve thrown themselves on the ground before God, humbled themselves, and sought His mercy and forgiveness. What we do know is that they didn't. Instead of being transparent, Adam and Eve decided to hide their problems and handle them by themselves. Thousands of years later we're still doing the same thing.

In chapter 1 we went over the destructive cycle the original narcissist, Satan, employed to gain power over Adam and Eve in the Garden of Eden. Again, this cycle is:

deception → *doubt* → *disobedience* → *dread* → which led to their spiritual *death*

Today, using a narcissist or multiple narcissists in your life, Satan continues to target you exactly where you are, using the same old tactic he used with Adam and Eve. With an unbeliever he uses the formula we covered earlier. For a child of God, Satan tweaks his formula from ending in spiritual death to one that results in living a life marked by defeat. In other words, if he can't destroy you completely, he will make sure you walk around feeling constantly defeated. Throughout this chapter we'll go over the strategy Satan employs against you in using a narcissist to lead you to a life of defeat.

The road map to your healing starts with answering that same question God asked Adam back in Genesis 3: "Where are you?" This question isn't meant to induce shame or condemnation but to prompt self-reflection. To break free from any destructive cycle, it's crucial to be honest with yourself and recognize the traps you're currently stuck in. This is similar to embarking on a road trip to a place you've never been to and using your current location as a starting point in a GPS.

For a child of God, the strategy Satan employs is:

deception → *doubt* → *disobedience* → *dread* → *defeat*

Using the four common traps as a basis, we'll uncover exactly how the enemy entraps you and how the destructive cycle plays out in each trap.

Knowing which trap(s) you're currently stuck in is half the equation. The other half is understanding how you got there and how to guard your heart from Satan's future schemes against you, which we will cover throughout the remainder of the book.

Following are the four traps we fall into as a result of narcissistic abuse. As you read through them, ask the Lord to open your eyes and heart and reveal which one you're in. A word of caution: When you reach this step, it's common for the enemy to distract you by pointing out which trap someone you know is stuck in, to keep you from following through in your own healing process. If, as you're reading this, you notice that someone you know fits this category, take note of it. You can talk to them about it later. But for now, stay focused on the journey you've started.

Trap 1: Self-Defeat

People who commonly fall into this trap tend to value relationships. The enemy sweeps in early in their lives—often between God's identity declaration and their early developmental formation (through age nineteen)—to get them into this cycle. As a result of the rejection they endured at the hands of a narcissist, they're in denial of their need for love and have written themselves off as unlovable and turned to other means to feel OK. Those means can be people who aren't good for them, substances, or spiritual methods such as Reiki, crystals, and so forth that they use in a desperate attempt to calm the storm within and achieve internal peace. People who fall into this trap often possess a God-given ability to empathize with others, which the enemy uses to his advantage.

If you find yourself caught in the trap of self-defeat, your enemy likely used a narcissistic person in your life to spew condemnation your way during a vulnerable period in your life. Because we tend to fall into this as a result of developmental-years trauma (through age nineteen), the narcissist was likely either an authority figure or a peer. The enemy used someone you had or have relational currency with, because the closer you are to someone, the lower your guard is. This made you more likely to believe the words they said about you as truth.

Deceived by that person's words or actions toward you, combined with a lack of understanding of God's love and pursuit of you, *doubt* entered your heart. You began to believe that your worth was at the mercy of that person's opinion of you. Since that person was driven by Satan, who's been studying you your whole life, the narcissist knew exactly what to say for his words to cut deep into your heart.

After listening to the narcissist's words long enough, combined with your lack of knowledge of truth

(Hos. 4:6), you began to condemn yourself with the very words the narcissist spoke over you, calling yourself stupid, ugly, or whatever labels they put on you. At this point you don't need anyone to criticize you; you've become the devil's mouthpiece to yourself. Since you hold the criticism spoken over you as truth, when someone comes along and tells you God loves you or cares about you, you likely respond to God's love with doubt and push that person away because you've already written yourself off.

Even in times when you try to believe the truth, it just doesn't seem to take root. It feels as if there's a disconnect between what you know God says about you and how you feel about yourself. Meanwhile, deep down your need for love doesn't go away, so you find other ways to meet this need, most likely by living in a way that contradicts who God made you to be, launching into a lifestyle of *disobedience*, whether by masking your pain with self-medicating or settling for any kind of attention because you don't believe you'll ever be loved.

Caught in a self-defeating cycle, you most likely feel ashamed about the lifestyle you're living. Anytime you try to get better, the words of the narcissist(s) in your life come back to haunt you. You feel haunted by their words, by your mistakes. You live in a constant state of *dread*. You can't remember the last time you were happy. The last time you felt safe. The last time you felt comfortable in your own skin. You know God is holy; you also see Him as someone who is far away. Someone who is disappointed in you. Someone who looks at you and shakes His head. Convinced you're defective beyond repair, you resort to living depressed, anxious, tormented, and most of all *defeated*.

TRAP 2: REBELLION

People who commonly fall for this trap have given up on the idea of extracting love from others. Their fear of rejection is so great they deny their need for love altogether and put all their focus on protecting themselves. They tend to have strong personalities. They have boldness, and because of their determination they possess a God-given ability to influence those around them.

In my experience as a counselor I've noticed that those who likely get stuck in a trap of rebellion have the capacity to break through social norms and influence beyond their direct circle. Their tenacity has the capacity to create a lasting impact in the lives of those around them. The enemy, however, uses their strong personalities to draw negative attention, which leads to them experiencing further rejection.

If you find yourself caught in the trap of rebellion, here's how it happened: To shortchange you, the enemy likely swept in years ago using a narcissist who made you feel as if no matter how hard you tried, you fell short. This can be the case of an authority figure who holds you to an unbearable standard or a peer who expects you to act just like them to be accepted—but because you stand your ground, they hurt you and turn others against you.

Or it could be the case where a protégé hurts you by betraying you.

The lie the narcissist *deceived* you into believing is that your value comes from behaving a certain way. In the beginning you may have tried to meet this person's high standards, but time after time it seemed that the harder you tried, the more you fell short, convincing you that there's nothing you can do for that person to ever accept you. Believing that your value comes from that person's acceptance, you fall into a cycle where you alternate between doubting your worth and being determined to prove you are worthy.

Either way, you feel the pain of falling short of unrealistic expectations over and over, and you give up on trying to please the narcissist in your life. Depending on who hurt you and what role they held, to try to stop further rejection, you rebel against those who remind you of the role that person played in your life. For example, if the narcissist who hurt you was an authority figure, you're likely to refuse direction from an authority figure, sometimes including God. If the narcissist was a peer, you're likely to isolate yourself from people in a peer role (for example, pushing friends away) to try to hide your vulnerabilities. If that person was a protégé, you're likely to become weary of those who ask you for help so as not to be taken advantage of again.

Having determined that you must have your own back, you automatically enter the *doubt* phase, where you doubt that even God cares about you and watches over you. Your flesh kicks in and you lead a lifestyle of *disobedience*, in which you choose to rely on yourself and trust in yourself because you think, "At least I won't let myself down!"

Depending on the depth of the hurt you endured throughout your life, you may even resort to denying you have any needs and therefore don't seek support out of fear you'll be hurt again. Though you may have convinced yourself you don't have needs, your needs don't go away—you just starve yourself in a desperate act of self-protection. The problem is, while you're starving yourself, the enemy comes in with a good-looking solution to your problem, often in the form of something that promises self-reliance in order to take care of yourself and never have to rely on someone else.

Enticed by the opportunity to prove yourself, you take the bait. Since you were never meant to shoulder your own weight, when you fall short, you judge yourself based on your own merit. You feel *dread* toward yourself for not meeting the standards you've set for yourself and hold those whose standards you're continuously striving to meet in contempt. Because God didn't intend for you to strive for your worth, you lack peace, and you may feel resentful, angry, tormented, and *defeated*.

Trap 3: Over-Accommodating

People who fall into this trap often value love and protection. The enemy plants critical and generally unhappy people in their lives, causing their sense of security to become shaky. This creates a strong desire for security, leading them to get stuck in a trap where they prioritize feeling secure and protected over feeling loved. People who fall into this trap have a God-given characteristic of being giving, but the enemy uses their God-given attribute to get them to try to earn love through service.

If this resonates with you, here's how you fell into this trap: Your enemy *deceived* you into believing that your inner security depends on the happiness of those around you. This habit may have started at an early age when the enemy perhaps enticed an authority figure in your life (someone you depended on for your sense of security) to wreak havoc on your sense of peace.

Whether that person constantly criticized you or was constantly agitated, or they projected explosive anger out of nowhere, feeling out of control, you made it your lifelong goal to regain some kind of control over your environment by keeping peace at any cost, which in your case was inner turmoil. Living in this trap for so long, you took on the role of peacekeeper even among your peers. Now you've developed a hypersensitivity to people's emotions and are able to sense the environment you've just walked into, and when you sense chaos, fear creeps in. *Doubting* God's willingness to take care of you, you quickly roll up your sleeves and get to work. By that I mean you start working on making the grumpy person happy—all in an attempt to restore the sense of harmony you so badly crave.

In your pursuit of inner security, you lead a life of *disobedience* in which you expend so much energy on peacekeeping and over-accommodating the needs of those around you. At times you may even justify your behavior as God's work. The problem with over-accommodating is that because you've put a yoke on your back you were never meant to carry, you begin to *dread* the very people you over-accommodate because nothing you do for them is ever good enough or appreciated. But because your sense of security is tied to them, you fear that if you stop over-accommodating them, they will reject you. So you find a way to justify your behavior in an attempt to calm the inner turmoil in your heart and mind.

If you fall into the trap of over-accommodating, the enemy may even throw in a protégé who is a narcissist as well. Because he knows you evaluate yourself based on how others see you, if you carry this mindset into your parenting, the enemy knows you are likely to raise someone he can entice to become a narcissist. In your attempt to make sure your child is well pleased and happy with you, the enemy will entice that child to believe the world revolves around them and must cater to them to the capacity you do. Now, because you were never meant to be a load-bearing wall for anyone, or to be in control but rather turn over your uncertainty to God, carrying the heavy burden of making sure others are happy leads you to a life of resentment and guilt-driven behavior—in other words, a life marked by *defeat*.

TRAP 4: ARROGANCE

People commonly fall into this trap via one of two avenues. The first is that they're brought up in environments where they are treated as if they're the sun and everything revolves around them. Because we're born with a fallen nature that seeks to exalt our will over God's will, being raised in an environment where we're told we are the greatest thing since sliced bread only exacerbates this nature and causes us to expect people to exalt us. The second avenue is that the person harboring resentment from unprocessed hurt is overcompensating through self-inflation, suppressing their insecurities while projecting a grandiose persona.

Either way this person deceives themself into believing they're entitled to special treatment. Unlike the other three traps, this one causes a person to doubt their need for God, not because they doubt God's ability to love them, as in the case of one who falls into the trap of self-defeat, or because they doubt they can achieve the proper level for God to accept them, as in the case of the rebel, nor because they doubt God can take care of them, as in the case of the over-accommodator. The one who falls into the trap of arrogance flat out doubts and therefore rejects their need for God because they believe they are entitled to special treatment, honor, and praise. In other words, in their hearts they've determined they are a god.

Because of this they lead a life of disobedience in which they build their own sense of identity on the backs of other people, either by requiring others to serve and acknowledge them to the capacity they feel they are entitled, or by putting people down in an attempt to elevate themselves. Driven by the need to feel superior, they dread anyone and anything that doesn't serve them, including God. Unfortunately, if the person (who is most likely an unbeliever) does not turn from this direction, their trajectory is spiritual death.

Now, there are times when someone stuck in the arrogance trap does end up coming out of it. Take a look at Saul of Tarsus, for example. Before he became Paul, Saul was bold, took aggressive measures, and had a reputation as a cruel man. Right before his conversion, the Book of Acts records:

> Meanwhile, Saul was still breathing out murderous threats against the Lord's disciples. He went to the high priest and asked him for letters to the synagogues in Damascus, so that if he found any there who belonged to the Way, whether men or women, he might take them as prisoners to Jerusalem....
>
> In Damascus there was a disciple named Ananias. The Lord called to him in a vision, "Ananias!" "Yes, Lord," he answered. The Lord told him, "Go to the house of Judas on Straight Street and ask for a man from Tarsus named Saul, for he is praying. In a vision he has seen a man named Ananias come and place his hands on him to restore his sight." "Lord," Ananias answered, "I have heard many reports about this man and all the harm he has done to your holy people in Jerusalem. And he has come here with authority from the chief priests to arrest all who call on your name."
>
> —Acts 9:1–2, 10–14

In other words, Ananias was thinking, "Lord, do You know who this man is? You're asking me to sign my own death warrant!" Acts 9:15 states, "But the Lord said to Ananias, 'Go! This man is my chosen instrument to proclaim my name to the Gentiles and their kings and to the people of Israel.'" The now converted Paul ended up boldly proclaiming the gospel of Jesus Christ to the nations. The Lord used his God-given characteristics for the good of the kingdom. This goes to show that in Christ we have the ability to crucify the flesh with all its desires and by His power get out of any demonic trap the enemy has set for us, whether we're foot-deep, knee-deep, or spiritually dead. The God who called Lazarus out of the grave is the One calling you out of your grave today.

The steps outlined in the rest of the book are clinically proven to help you heal from any narcissistic abuse you endured, no matter how severe. However, the steps in themselves carry no power. Deliverance is an act of God, commissioned by the Lord Jesus Christ. Stepping into your healing journey requires faith and diligence—faith that it is the Lord Jesus Christ alone who is your Deliverer. In the counseling room I make a point to my patients that I am not their deliverer. I am like one of the people Jesus commanded to remove the graveclothes from Lazarus. The Holy Spirit carries the power.

Walking in freedom also requires diligence to reject any falsehood the enemy will try to whisper in your ear throughout your healing journey. Some common ways the enemy will try to derail you is by whispering things such as, "This isn't going to work," "You've tried stuff like this before," and "How do you even know you're doing this right?" These lies are meant to induce doubt. Remember, doubt is one of his weapons. When you resist him, he'll try to induce fear by saying, "What if you mess with the kingdom of darkness, and the demons overpower you?" Scare tactics such as these are meant to get you to back down, because the enemy knows his time is limited and his influence is being broken in Jesus' name!

Other common ways I've witnessed in the counseling room are distractions. The person will start talking about topics that have nothing to do with the issue they need to be delivered from. At first I thought it was a coincidence. However, when this happened with one patient after another, I realized it was a tactic of the enemy to keep the person bound. Other ways include shaming you by reminding you of something from your past and either threatening to expose it to get you to back down or using the event to convince you that your healing isn't real because God is still mad at you about it.

One of his last straws at keeping you from moving forward is to use physical symptoms such as sudden headaches, nausea, or other forms of physical illness. These are last-ditch efforts to delay your breakthrough. If those should happen, resist, resist, and resist! Don't stop and get in a spewing match with the enemy. That also is a tactic. Instead, resist him, keep your eyes forward, follow the steps throughout the remainder of the chapters—and watch the deliverance of the Lord in your life.

Chapter 7

OVERTURNING DECEPTION

As we have covered so far, the original narcissist, Satan, is the one responsible for all narcissistic abuse. The Bible is clear that our fight is not against people but against spiritual forces of darkness (Eph. 6:12).

To effectively fight back, it's important to understand that the source of your pain is not solely the person Satan is using, although they are responsible for their actions. The true source of your pain is Satan and his demons.

First Peter 5:8–9 tells us to stay vigilant because the devil, our adversary, prowls like a lion, seeking whom he may devour. Satan, who desired to be like the Most High, fell from glory and now directs his hatred toward God's image bearers, which includes you—just as if someone who tried to harm you and couldn't would likely turn to those you love and try to harm them. When Satan couldn't harm God, he went after God's most precious possessions, His image bearers. In the Garden of Eden he targeted Adam and Eve and enticed them to doubt God's goodness, which led them to disobey Him.

Thankfully, long before the fall, God made provisions for you and me to be reconciled back to Him as our Father. When you and I give our lives to Jesus, God seals us with His Holy Spirit (Eph. 1:4) so we can use our free will to live for Him. The problem remains, however, that you live in a fallen world, combined with the fact that you were made to be in a dependent relationship with God, meaning your identity and purpose come from Him. Satan knows that without an active relationship with God, you would feel the void in your life left by the fall of our first parents. So he positioned people and opportunities in your life to fill that void. This way you would settle for a substitute.

In my experience treating patients who have suffered from narcissistic abuse, I have noticed a common thread: *They all held beliefs about themselves that contradicted what God said about them.* There hasn't been one patient in my history of treating, observing, and consulting on cases of narcissistic abuse who didn't share in that common thread. By holding on to beliefs about ourselves that contradict what God says about us, we feel insecure about who we are, and in desperation to find love and protection somewhere, we fall into one of the enemy's traps. When we do, we end up feeling helpless to the narcissistic abuse we endure.

Early in my career as a therapist, I focused on

therapeutic methods that were specifically successful for helping people who endured trauma, including narcissistic abuse. As I thought about why those methods were successful in the long term, rather than giving the patient short-term relief until the next problem happened, I realized a common thread: They addressed the root beliefs held by the patients that bore all the unhealthy emotions. The process I'm going to take you through is similar, except instead of dealing with one narcissistic abuse issue at a time, you will have the road map to overcoming all past narcissistic abuse, dealing with present residue from the abuse, and protecting yourself from future narcissistic abuse.

The reason our attempts to heal from narcissistic abuse often don't work—or if they do, they don't last past that one relationship—is that we try to tackle the problem in front of us rather than taking our time to find the root of the problem.

Healing from narcissistic abuse requires patience, prayer, and discernment. It also requires us to see the situation from a spiritual perspective. It necessitates pulling back the curtain and exposing the one pulling the strings, the one who's had a target on our backs since the beginning of humanity—Satan.

In the previous chapter you identified the trap(s) most applicable to you. Regardless of whichever trap you resonate with, your first step is to contradict the deception the enemy planted in your heart that made you susceptible to narcissistic abuse so you can fill yourself with the truth. The truth is, you were made in God's image, meaning that within you are characteristics that represent God, and that after the fall you inherited a sinful nature, so naturally you try to live apart from Him. God created you to be complete in Him. You were made for a daily relationship with Him where you talk to Him and include Him in your daily decisions—in other words, a life submitted to Him as your Creator, your God, and your Father, and in which you draw your identity from Him.

To hurt you, the enemy capitalizes on your sinful nature, which doesn't naturally seek after God, and sweeps in using a narcissist to fill your void. Once you fall for the trick, the enemy uses that person to give you a negative frame of reference about relationships so that at best, when it comes to your relationship with God, you'll likely see Him as someone who's far from you, someone who's angry in general or angry with you, or someone who's indifferent to you. As long as you see God in one of those lights, you'll never allow yourself to get close enough to Him to draw your identity from Him.

I mean, think about it: If you believe God can't be trusted, then you more than likely are not going to draw close to Him. You may "do religion," but you will not allow yourself to get close enough to have a close relationship with Him as your loving Father, which would require you to be vulnerable with Him and trust Him.

A lot of times we don't know which lies we believe about God until we bring them up to the surface. There have been times when I've had patients bring me questions and doubts they had about God that they didn't feel comfortable bringing up to their pastor because they were afraid their pastor would see them as a "bad Christian." As we navigated through their doubts and questions, I could see the relief in their eyes when they were in a space where they could ask those questions. I would sit down with them, and we would bring all their doubts out on the table because when we expose and deal with the lies, the enemy can no longer successfully use those lies to influence us.

So the first step to arming yourself against narcissistic abuse is to overturn the deception planted in your heart by the enemy long ago, deception dealing with lies you currently believe about God and keeping you from clinging to Him alone as your source of identity.

Throughout the remainder of the chapter, I'm going to go over the common lies victims of narcissistic abuse tend to believe about God that keep them from clinging to Him as their source, leaving no room for the enemy's deceit.

As you go through each one, pray that God will open your eyes to the lies the enemy has deceived you into believing about Him.

Lie 1: God Doesn't Have My Best Interest at Heart

This lie is as old as creation. It's the same lie Satan used to deceive Eve into doubting God's intention, leading her to go against God's command. The reality is as we've already established. God didn't need us; He wanted us. Genesis 1:26 says, "God said, 'Let us make mankind in our image, in our likeness, so that they may rule over the fish in the sea and the birds in the sky, over the livestock and all the wild animals, and over all the creatures that move along the ground.'"

After God made Adam and Eve, He gave them authority. Then God blessed them (v. 28), provided for them (v. 29), and gave them a sense of purpose (Gen. 2:15). And even after Adam and Eve went against God's command, He still covered them (Gen. 3:21), foreshadowing the future covering He would provide for us through Jesus, who would remove our sins as far as the east is from the west and restore us to the status He intended for us to have as sons and daughters. Why in the world would someone who doesn't have our best interest go through all that trouble?

LIE 2: GOD IS NEVER HAPPY WITH ME

I found that this belief resonated with those stuck in the traps of self-defeat, rebellion, and over-accommodating. We fall into this deception when we heed the enemy's whisper, "You need to earn God's love by being perfect." You see, deception is rarely a blatant lie, which is obvious to spot. Deception is a lie sprinkled with some truth, making it harder to decipher. To deceive us, the enemy presents to us the idea that God is indeed holy and perfect, yet he omits the fact that God is also loving and merciful and that His pursuit of us is driven by His love for us. Once we fall for the lie that God is never happy with us, Satan reinforces it by planting people in our lives who are never satisfied with us.

God's Word is clear that in Jesus, He chose us, He justified us, and one day He will glorify us. God grants us a right standing with Him and sees us as His children whom He loves. God's love for you is revealed through His pursuit of you. His pursuit is not based on your merit but because He is so loving and good—and out of His love for you He pursued you to have a relationship with Him.

Lie 3: God Wants to Use Me and Abuse Me

Unfortunately, this lie is planted through having been exploited by someone who was supposed to care for us. As a result, we see authority figures as a threat to our sense of security, making us react in a self-protective way toward God. Years ago I treated a patient who struggled with her relationship with God. She had been raised by a narcissistic parent, so she viewed God as just a bigger version of the narcissistic parent who raised her. My patient would get triggered by phrases such as, "You are here for God's plans and purposes," or, "Deny yourself and follow me," both of which, when used in the correct context, are meant to save us from our own self-destructive nature.

But when we've experienced the pain of betrayal that we haven't yet dealt with, Satan can swoop in and make these statements sound as though God just wants you to blindly surrender to Him so He can do whatever He wants with you to your detriment. The reality is that God wants us to live in a relationship with Him so we can receive the truth of who we are (a principle we will cover in a few chapters). And out of this truth, we will be able to recognize the deceiver's lies, take authority over them, and close the door to further narcissistic abuse in our lives.

Lie 4: God Could Never Love Me

This is one of the most heartbreaking lies we fall for. Many of us act as if we don't believe it, but the reality is, deep down we question whether God truly *is* with and for us because we feel unworthy of it. It's common for individuals trapped in over-accommodating to fall for this lie. As a counselor, you wouldn't believe how often someone has asked me, "Why would God love me? I'm not worthy of it." To that I answer, "None of us are worthy of God's love. God didn't choose to love us because we somehow earned His love. Out of the goodness of His heart He chose to seek us out. To take us in. To clean us up and fill us with His love for us. There is nothing you can do to make God love you more than He already does, because His love for you didn't begin with your works [Eph 1:5] and therefore is not contingent on your works [Isa. 64:6]."

Lie 5: God Just Wants to Control Me

This is one of the most popular deceptions people, including me, have fallen into at some point. This belief stems from an unhealed wound in which you felt controlled or helpless. As a result, you see God as someone who only cares about you following rules and regulations, rather than one who cares about healing your heart.

The Bible is clear that even our best works are filthy rags when compared with the holiness of God. And unlike what other religions teach, there's nothing we could have done on our own to reach a status worthy enough for God. Why? Because as you recall back in Genesis, our status, or worth, was given to us by God and attached to our relationship with Him. I've had many patients who were apprehensive about submitting to God for fear they'd become subjected to an unbearable load of rules. This lie goes back to legalism. God has already satisfied the standard on your behalf in Jesus. Now God gives you, as His child, the Holy Spirit to lead you, guide you, and protect you from the enemy's lies.

Understanding that God's guardrails are for our own protection comes with time as we learn to fellowship with the Holy Spirit and get to know the Father's heart for us from our own relationship with Him, rather than from how someone else mis-portrayed Him to us.

Lie 6: I Don't Need God

This belief can be a reactive stance that stems from an unhealed wound in which a person felt betrayed so they made a vow to rely on themselves only, as in the case of someone stuck in the cycle of rebellion. This can also be a stance someone takes when they've been treated with an overwhelming amount of praise and adoration. They've convinced themselves they're god, and therefore they won't submit to God, as in the case of someone stuck in the arrogance trap.

After rescuing the Israelites out of the hands of Pharaoh, God showed them His fatherly love by providing for them miraculously, and when they were attacked, He showed them just how much their victory relied on Him. In reading Scripture, you see how God is the One who grants victory. Look at this account of when a group of people called the Amalekites attacked the Israelites:

> The Amalekites came and attacked the Israelites at Rephidim. Moses said to Joshua, "Choose some of our men and go out to fight the Amalekites. Tomorrow I will stand on top of the hill with the staff of God in my hands." So Joshua fought the Amalekites as Moses had ordered, and Moses, Aaron and Hur went to the top of the hill. As long as Moses held up his hands, the Israelites were winning, but whenever he lowered his hands, the Amalekites were winning.
>
> —Exodus 17:8–11

How can you explain something like this? Coincidence? You see, this battle took place not long after God had delivered the Israelites out of the hands of Pharaoh. The Israelites had been enslaved for so long that God was showing them not only that He was their source of security, as when He fed them manna from heaven (Exod. 16), but time after time He was also their source of victory. The story continues in verses 12–13:

> When Moses' hands grew tired, they took a stone and put it under him and he sat on it. Aaron and Hur held his hands up—one on one side, one on the other—so that his hands remained steady till sunset. So Joshua overcame the Amalekite army with the sword.

The same truth applies to us today. Our victory begins and ends with God.

My favorite way of reading God's Word is using a chronological Bible because I can see a pattern of His faithful love as I follow through the historical accounts. Regardless of how many times you read through Scripture, the enemy will try to come up with new ways to deceive you into believing that God doesn't have your best interest at heart, or that God is just trying to use and abuse you, or that He wants to control you. This is a tactic Satan uses to get your flesh nature to kick into gear so you'll try to secure your own sense of love and protection outside God's will. And when you do, he can have his way with you.

As you read God's Word, however, you realize that even through our unfaithfulness to Him, God has remained faithful to us. He comes after us and time and time again proves to us that He is where our healing is. He is who our hearts have yearned for all our lives. *He* is our home.

Scripture bears witness to God's mercy. The Book of 1 Kings recalls a time when God sent the prophet Elijah to pronounce judgment on King Ahab (Jezebel's husband) because of all the evil he had done: "When Ahab heard these words [of God's judgment], he tore his clothes, put on sackcloth and fasted. He lay in sackcloth and went around meekly" (21:27). When Ahab responded with genuine repentance to the Lord, "then the word of the LORD came to Elijah the Tishbite: 'Have you noticed how Ahab has humbled himself before me? Because he has humbled himself, I will not bring this disaster in his day'" (vv. 28–29). In response to genuine repentance, God was willing to show mercy to even the most evil king.

"WHERE WAS GOD?"

Before we learn how to overturn deceptions we've held about God, I want to touch on a topic I've been asked about almost every time I've treated a patient who has endured narcissistic abuse. The question is, "Where was God when I was getting abused?" If the abuse happened when you were young, I can assure you God was right there with you. The fact that He allowed it to happen does not negate His love for you. I promise you that if you choose to trust in His love for you, you will see how He will use your experience for good somehow, someway.

As a counselor, I don't get to talk about myself or share my stories much because I try to keep the focus on the patient I'm treating. So many times my patients have looked at me from the perspective of where I am today and seen someone who has it all together. The reality is that apart from the grace of God, I don't know where I'd be. The reason I specialized in trauma counseling is that I've gone through my own series of traumas, hurts, and betrayals that I myself have taken to the throne room of the Father time and time again and asked the same question my patients are afraid to ask: "Why did You let me go through ____________?"

As I've come to know the Father's heart and walked with Him, I've realized that God was there through every trial, and I've chosen to lay my wall down and trust that He allowed it for a reason. God has been faithful to show me how He's used the pain in my life to help me empathize with those going through pain. He's used the pain in my life to keep me from trusting in myself. Most of all, He's used the pain in my life to wean me off what this world has to offer. Through the pain I've learned how fickle people can be, how deceitful my own heart can be, and how faithful He is because when He was the only one I had, I realized that He alone is enough.

The reason I'm so passionate about you understanding God's true nature is that I've seen how the enemy has used our lack of knowledge about God's true nature to keep us from drawing close to Him, so instead we look toward the wrong people and things and stay bound.

Regardless of which trap you've identified with, the first step to your healing begins the same: by removing the enemy's authority over you. You do this in three separate steps that I will outline in the subsequent chapters.

The first step deals with ownership. Plainly stated, you either belong to the devil or you belong to Jesus. There are no in-betweens. The devil may have deceived you into believing that you belong to yourself because you do as you see fit. That's not biblical. I've had patients who asked if they could undergo deliverance without submitting to Jesus as Lord. My answer is that I wouldn't recommend it because unless you're under the authority of Christ, this is what Jesus says will happen to you post-deliverance,

> When an impure spirit comes out of a person, it goes through arid places seeking rest and does not find it. Then it says, "I will return to the house I left." When it arrives, it finds the house unoccupied, swept clean and put in order [this is an unbeliever's post-deliverance status]. Then the impure spirit goes and takes with it seven other spirits more wicked than itself, and they go in and live there. And the final condition of that person is worse than the first.
>
> —MATTHEW 12:43–45

In a parallel passage, Jesus said, "When a strong man, fully armed, guards his own house, his possessions are safe. But when someone stronger attacks and overpowers him, he takes away the armor in which the man trusted and divides up his plunder" (Luke 11:21–22). From these passages you can see that as a person, you belong either to the kingdom of darkness or to Jesus. The only way to issue the devil an eviction notice is to proclaim to him that you are under new ownership—the ownership of Your Lord and Savior, Jesus Christ. Once you do this, the Holy Spirit of the living God indwells you, marking you as God's child. And He is greater than any powers of darkness.

To submit to the lordship of Jesus Christ, pray this prayer by faith:

> *Lord Jesus, I acknowledge that I am a sinner and in need of a Savior. Thank You for dying on the cross for me. Please forgive me for all my sins. Thank You for being my Lord and Savior. Thank You for sealing me with the Holy Spirit. Please help me live in a way that is pleasing to You. Amen.*

Chapter 8

CRUSHING DOUBT

Now that the ownership issue is dealt with, we're ready to start inner work to strengthen you from the inside out and arm you against future narcissistic abuse. The first house my husband and I owned was a fixer-upper. Purchasing a fixer-upper comes with a commitment where you know there's a lot of work to do, but you always keep in mind the vision of what the house will become once the work is done.

As you go through this process, hold on to a vision of the end result: the freedom you get to live in to be everything God intended for you to be. There will be times when the enemy will whisper doubt in your mind to make you question whether God is with you; in those times I want you to remember that He is with you and He has promised that He began a good work in you and is faithful to complete it (Phil. 1:6). God is the new owner of the house, and He is faithful to not throw in the towel on you. Your job is to keep fighting the good fight of faith.

Your next step deals with renouncing the lies the enemy has planted in your heart about who God is. Declaring the truth about Him is such an important step because it deals with uprooting seeds of doubt that led you to fall into the narcissistic abuse to begin with and replacing them with the truth.

To complete this step, say the following prayer out loud and in faith:

> *Faithful Father, I confess that through the years, I've held on to beliefs about You that are not true. Please forgive me and cleanse my mind from all unbelief.*
>
> *Father, I renounce the lie that You don't have my best interest at heart.*
>
> *Father, thank You that in Jesus, You've shown me that You have looked out for me before I was even born.*
>
> *I renounce the lie that You want to use me and abuse me.*
>
> *Thank You, Father, for seeking me out and giving me the status of being Your child, through Jesus.*
>
> *I renounce the lie that You just want to control me.*

Thank You, Father, for guiding me with Your protective love. Thank You for giving me Your Word and the Holy Spirit to guide, teach, comfort, and convict me.

I renounce the lie that I don't need You in my life.

Lord Jesus, I declare that You are the Lord of my life. Give me an undivided heart that seeks to follow You alone.

I renounce the lie that bad situations are Your way of punishing me for past sins.

Thank You, Father, that if I confess my sins, You are faithful to forgive me and to cleanse me from all unrighteousness.

I renounce the lie that I am not doing enough to keep You happy with me.

Thank You, Father, that the basis of my relationship with You isn't my works but the finished work of my Lord and Savior, Jesus Christ. Thank You that in Jesus, You accept me as Your child.

I renounce the lie that You're just about done with me.

Thank You, Father, that Your mercies are new every morning. Thank You that You are faithful to complete the work You have begun in me.

I renounce the lie that You are mad at me.

Thank You, Father, that in Christ Jesus, nothing can ever separate me from Your love.

I renounce the lie that You're too busy with bigger things to hear me.

Thank You, Father, that I can bring my cares and concerns to You. Thank You that in Jesus, I am not an orphan but Your child. Thank You for guiding me by Your Holy Spirit.

Father, please search my heart and reveal to me the lies I've been believing that have kept me from trusting You completely.

Be patient as the Holy Spirit reveals deceptions to you. As He does, continue to renounce. For example, if you've believed that God is harsh, renounce it by saying, "I renounce the lie that You are harsh," and search Scripture to cling to the truth about who He is.

Remember, if the enemy doesn't attack your perspective of God, he will try to make you doubt God's love for you. Recognize it as an enemy attack. Don't entertain it. Don't listen to it. Listening means hearing something and acting upon what you heard. You may not be able to help what he whispers, but you can help what you receive from him. Once you hear his lies, don't accept them as the truth. Instead, renounce them and speak God's truth over you.

Now that you've renounced lies and declared the truth about God, your next step is to replace doubt with faith. Doing so requires identifying and renouncing the substitutes the enemy has used in your life to get you to settle for something or someone other than God.

God substitutes are also known as idols and can

take on many forms. These can be other religions or belief systems, spiritual practices, people, and things. Throughout counseling I've found that some idols are easier to spot than others because while some are obvious, others hide behind the veil of things that are socially acceptable.

Idolatry is the greatest form of betrayal. It is described by God as "breaking faith with God" by putting our trust in someone or something other than Him. It is our utterly rejecting the One who died for us and instead choosing to follow after the enemy Jesus died to save us *from* by fulfilling ourselves with anything and anyone but Him.

One of the most distressing passages in the Bible is found in Jeremiah 2. It's distressing because it's so relevant to the pattern we fall into today. This passage expresses God's grief with the Israelites, who continually chose to follow after everyone and everything but Him. Yet when all their efforts to seek after other gods proved futile, they would cry out to God again and again. This time God was very upset with them, and rightly so. I mean, can you imagine the hurt of betrayal you would feel pledging your commitment to someone who continually chose someone or something else over you?

In Jeremiah 2:13 God said: "My people have committed two sins: They have forsaken me, the spring of living water, and have dug their own cisterns, broken cisterns that cannot hold water." In other words, they turned their allegiance from God and tried to fulfill themselves using means that could never fulfill them.

Jeremiah 2:27–28 says,

> They have turned their backs to me and not their faces; yet when they are in trouble, they say, "Come and save us!" Where then are the gods you made for yourselves? Let them come if they can save you when you are in trouble! For you, Judah, have as many gods as you have towns.

This passage is a reminder that regardless of how many times the enemy presents us with an opportunity or a person to "complete" us, may we remember that no number of idols can fill God's place in our lives: no job, no relationship or any other idol can.

Completing this step requires that we identify what we put our trust in to feel secure. We'll start with obvious forms of idolatry and work our way toward the more subtle idols that make us susceptible to narcissistic abuse.

Religious Practices

Acts 19:19–20 reminds us to repent of and renounce previous religious practices we've engaged in.

> Many of those who believed now came and openly confessed what they had done. A number who had practiced sorcery brought their scrolls together and burned them publicly. When they calculated the value of the scrolls, the total came to fifty thousand drachmas. In this way the word of the Lord spread widely and grew in power.

Through the years, I've treated many Christians who after they gave their lives to Jesus continued to struggle with mindsets and belief systems rooted in other religious practices. When asked if they ever renounced their dealings with past religious practices, the answer 90 percent of the time was no—not because they didn't want to but because they didn't know they needed to.

Growing up Muslim, part of the school curriculum required me to memorize Quran verses. Years later, as a believer, those verses remained stuck in my mind. There were times when the verses would resurface and replay in my mind. The problem was that the Quran blasphemes Jesus, so when those verses would replay in my mind, I'd get afraid and start doubting my salvation. It took me years to realize this was one of the enemy's tactics. Once I renounced Islam and other practices and held on to God's Word, much like burning the scrolls and declaring your allegiance to Jesus alone, Quran verses stopped replaying in my mind.

First Kings 18 tells some of the actions of King Ahab. After he became king, Ahab built shrines to other gods, which eventually led the nation of Israel astray. Having one foot in and one foot out, Israel was confronted by the prophet Elijah about their split allegiance. Verse 21 says: "Elijah went before the people and said, 'How long will you waver between two opinions? If the Lord is God, follow him; but if Baal is God, follow him.'"

If you read the rest of this encounter, you see that God in His patience proved to Israel yet again that He is the one true God, whose power far exceeds any of the gods they had set up in their hearts. Placing our faith in God alone requires renouncing all other "gods" we've ever placed our faith in. To renounce past religious practices, say the following prayer by faith,

> *Lord Jesus, I declare my allegiance to You and You alone. Jesus, I confess that I've taken part in religious and spiritual practices. In Your presence I renounce my allegiance to them. Please show me which of these religious practices I've taken part in, whether knowingly or unknowingly, so that I may renounce them.*

Islam

Hinduism

Buddhism

Sikhism

Bahá'í

Jainism

Shinto Taoism

Zoroastrianism

Confucianism

Animism

Indigenous and tribal religions

Bön

Cao Dai

Tenrikyo

Rastafarianism

Scientology

Wicca

Atheism/agnosticism

Other: __________

Using this list, for each religious practice you've taken part in, say, "I renounce my allegiance to ______________________."

Spiritual Practices

Centuries ago the devil used Asherah poles and Baals to divide the allegiance of the Israelites. Over time the enemy has continued to use similar tactics to make us divide our loyalty between God and another object of faith.

There was a town in India that missionaries traveled to and preached the gospel. To their surprise, many people gave their lives to Jesus. The missionaries were so excited at the success of their mission work. Year after year the missionaries went back to India, only to realize that the reason great numbers of people were accepting Jesus as their Lord and Savior was that those very people were only adding Jesus to their existing list of gods. Jesus was just one more security blanket added to their list. Many of us may look at that and think, "Oh my goodness, I can't believe that!" when in reality we often fall into this very trap. We accept Jesus as an additional God to the existing gods in our lives.

An object of faith is anything you put your faith in, whether for guidance or protection, even if it's in addition to God. Throughout the course of counseling patients, I've come across so many people who didn't think twice about reading their horoscope, wearing crystals, or engaging in Reiki. Be careful of practices that seem harmless. I've listed common practices that open the door to the enemy in your life. I cover and expand more on the practices below in my book *The Three Enemies of Your Mental Health*:

- » Santeria
- » crystal healing
- » Reiki (energy healing)
- » shamanic journeying
- » Native American ceremonies and rituals
- » tarot card reading
- » palm reading
- » astrology and horoscope consultation
- » spirit guides
- » spirit animals
- » chakra balancing
- » breath work and pranayama
- » sound healing (using singing bowls, gongs, etc.)
- » druidry
- » astral projection

Using this list to renounce spiritual practices you've taken part in, say:

> *Lord Jesus, I confess that I have taken part in ____________________. I repent of doing that. Please forgive me. I cancel every spiritually*

binding vow I made with the enemy knowingly and unknowingly as a result of taking part in ____________________. Lord God, by Your Holy Spirit, please fill every void that this activity was filling. I trust You alone. Please guide me and teach me to discern Your voice. Amen.

After renouncing these practices, if you have tarot cards, crystals you've been using for protection or healing, or any other occult paraphernalia, throw it away.

Subtle Idols

Ever since the beginning of time God has instructed us to listen to Him and not heed any counsel that contradicts what He tells us, regardless of how close we are to the person who counsels us. Let's look at how one bad counsel can lead us down a destructive path.

In Genesis 2:17, God commanded Adam, "But you must not eat from the tree of the knowledge of good and evil, for when you eat from it you will certainly die." After the enemy got into Eve's head, Genesis 3:6 says, "When the woman saw that the fruit of the tree was good for food and pleasing to the eye, and also desirable for gaining wisdom, she took some and ate it. She also gave some to her husband, who was with her, and he ate it." After Adam sinned against God, God said to Adam, "Because you listened to your wife and ate fruit from the tree about which I commanded you, 'You must not eat from it,' cursed is the ground because of you" (Gen. 3:17).

From the beginning God made a point to show us that our allegiance must be to Him. Regardless of how great you think someone is, or how close you are to them, your allegiance must rest with God.

In treating narcissistic abuse, I've found that the most common reason a victim has a hard time detaching from someone they know is narcissistic and toxic to them is that at some point in their lives they elevated the narcissist to a status that only belongs to God. In other words, in their hearts they tie themselves to that person. As a result, the narcissist's criticism has the capacity to affect the victim's emotional health. I've even had patients who before stepping into their healing journey spent months and even years feeling tormented and helpless to the torment they were under.

When it comes to protecting yourself against narcissistic abuse, you have to make sure your allegiance is to God alone. There are times when God will test our allegiance as He did with Abraham. Abraham had a close relationship with God. When God called Abraham, He promised to bless him with a child, which Abraham and Sarah desperately wanted. If you've ever experienced infertility, you understand the longing to finally hold the baby you've dreamed of. In Abraham and Sarah's case, decades had passed by. Finally, Sarah became pregnant and gave birth to a son they named Isaac. Isaac was Abraham's pride and joy. After all, he was going to carry out Abraham's legacy. Genesis 22 recounts Abraham's testing as follows.

> Some time later God tested Abraham. He said to him, "Abraham!" "Here I am," he replied. Then God said, "Take your son, your only son, *whom you love—Isaac*—and go to the region of Moriah. Sacrifice him there as a burnt offering on a mountain I will show you."
>
> —Genesis 22:1–2, emphasis added

Now pay attention; God told Abraham to take his son, *whom he loved*. Compare that with what God instructed Moses to tell the Israelites after God delivered them out of their enemies' hands in Egypt.

After issuing the Ten Commandments, God repeated the first commandment a few verses later through Moses when he said, "Hear, O Israel: The Lord our God, the Lord is one. Love the Lord your God with all your heart and with all your soul and with all your strength" (Deut. 6:4–5). Now fast-forward to centuries later. Mark 12:28–30 recalls a conversation in which teachers of the law asked Jesus, "Of all the commandments, which is the most important?" "The most important one," answered Jesus, "is this: 'Hear, O Israel: The Lord our God, the Lord is one. Love the Lord your God with all your heart and with all your soul and with all your mind and with all your strength.'"

Going back to God telling Abraham to sacrifice his son, whom he loves, to Him, as you read through the remainder of the story, you see that God had no intention of Abraham actually sacrificing Isaac. His command was simply to test Abraham's heart to see who the object of worship truly was in his life: God or Isaac. The Creator or the gift. Genesis 22:11–12 says, "But the angel of the Lord called out to him from heaven, 'Abraham! Abraham!' 'Here I am,' he replied. 'Do not lay a hand on the boy,' he said. 'Do not do anything to him. Now I know that *you fear God*, because you have not withheld from me your son, your only son'" (emphasis added).

In this context the original Hebrew word for *fear* does not imply dread but rather reverence—the highest form of respect. In other words, Abraham held God up on the pedestal of his heart.

Similar to Abraham, and contrary to popular belief, God is not interested in taking people from your life or stuff from you. What God is most interested in is His position in your heart because He knows that by our hearts we are ruled and whatever takes precedence in our hearts will control our day-to-day decisions. The Bible says it this way: "For where your treasure is, there your heart will be also" (Matt. 6:21). Anyone or anything you depend on, attach yourself to, or put your worth in has the potential of becoming an idol. This is how the enemy can easily turn a gift—as in something God intended for good, such as motherhood or a ministry—into a god in our lives, something that becomes an object of worship.

The reason we often fall into the trap of looking to

man for a sense of security is that we're looking for something that's tangible. Something that's in front of us. Something that's going to fulfill us in the way we believe we need to be fulfilled. That's how the enemy was able to place the narcissist in our lives so intricately in a way we didn't even notice. He knew which voids we weren't filling with God, and he placed the narcissist strategically to fill those voids so that once we latched on, he had full control of us.

Dismantling an idol takes away its power from your life, which takes away the enemy's ability to use that idol to further influence you. To complete this step, I encourage you to get with God and ask Him to reveal any idols you've placed in your heart that have been competing with His place in your heart and renounce your allegiance to them. You can do this by saying the following prayer:

> *Father God, I confess that I have put people and things above You in my heart. Please forgive me. Teach me to open up to You without reservation, and show me who and what I have elevated in my heart above You.*

The following are signs that the people have become idols:

» You care about their opinion more than God's opinion.

» You compromise what you know God's Word says to appease them.

» You equate favor with them to emotional security.

» You believe that appeasing them will make you more favorable to God or get you closer to Him.

People who may easily be elevated to the role of idols in your life often include:

» a parent,

» a spouse,

» children,

» siblings,

» other family members,

» friends,

» a mentor,

» a boss,

» a pastor,

» or someone else: ____________________

The following are signs that something has become an idol:

- You compromise your values to attain or maintain it.
- You believe that ________________ makes you more secure or valuable.
- You believe that ______________makes you more favorable to God.

Things that may easily become an idol if we're not careful:

- money
- sports
- ministry/works
- self/reputation
- material possessions
- physical appearance
- job/status
- other: ___________

When God shows you, pray the following prayer by inserting each person or item by name:

> *Father, I confess that I have idolized ______________ in my life. I ask for Your forgiveness. I renounce my allegiance to ______________________. I declare my allegiance to You alone. Father, as I have*

renounced each idol from my life, by Your Spirit, please fill the void I was feeling with You and teach me to rely on You, trust in You, and discern Your voice. Amen.

Chapter 9

OVERCOMING DISOBEDIENCE

Now that we've dealt with declaring our allegiance to God and renouncing our allegiance to all other gods in our lives, including the allegiance we've shown the narcissist who's had a hold over us, we're ready for the next step—exchanging disobedience for submission. This is one of the toughest steps we have to go through because (1) it goes against our human nature, and (2) we're dealing with wounds that have likely been festering within us for many years.

Moving past the pain of our past requires that we not only acknowledge the existence of the pain but consciously expose it and entrust it into the hands of the One who loves us most. This is how we experience emotional freedom from the inner turmoil caused by narcissistic abuse—emotional freedom from the what-ifs and the should'ves, would'ves, and could'ves. This is how you break free from the grip of the past so it no longer affects your present and future—whether the abuse took place decades ago or yesterday.

The Necessity of Forgiveness

To step into this freedom, you have to be willing to forgive the narcissist for what they did to you and for the hurt and pain they caused you. Before we jump into this step, I want to clarify that though your responsibility as a child of God is to forgive, it does not imply an obligation to reconcile with your offender. We forgive out of reverence for God, because that's what God told us to do, and because we submit to His will, we crucify our own desire to seek revenge and instead forgive the offender. Forgiveness is between you and God. The enemy wants nothing more than to convince us not to forgive, because he knows unforgiveness gives him a foothold in our lives.

There have been times in my life when I opened my heart to people, only for them to hurt me. When this happens, we're supposed to go to God about it, cry out to Him, forgive the people, and move forward by setting healthy boundaries. Although I knew this, I continued to hold a grudge because it made me feel protected against future hurt. The problem was that by insisting on protecting myself, I stepped out of alignment with God's will, and as a result, I felt tormented by the pain of the past. Matthew 18:21–37 shows that if we don't forgive, we're acting in rebellion toward God, and therefore God turns us over to our tormentors.

In my case the enemy tormented me with thoughts about those people, including how much I couldn't stand them. How dare they hurt me! I tried to prove to myself that I was worthy and that I wasn't who they labeled me to be. Looking back, I had fallen into the very trap the enemy set out for me. I took my eyes off Jesus and instead put them on myself and those who had hurt me. As a result, I wasted so much time trying to prove I was better than how they had perceived me. I took the words they used to describe me as motivation to prove I was the exact opposite of how they labeled me. And for what?

None of my efforts changed their perception of me. It only made me tired, anxious, and frustrated. One day, in frustration, I cried out to God and asked Him to release me from the torment I was caught up in. God reminded me of His command to forgive. So I humbled myself and forgave my perpetrators. I promise you, not even five minutes later the anxiety and panic left my mind—to the point where I texted some of my closest friends and shared the news with them because I was amazed at the power of God.

You, child of God, have access to that same power. Your responsibility is to walk out James 4:7, which says submit to God, resist the devil, and he will flee from you. Again, I'm not saying you need to reconcile with your perpetrators. Your responsibility is to forgive those who have hurt you.

As you step into this freedom, I pray in the mighty name of Jesus that every demonic spirit that has been tormenting you will crumble in fear at the presence of the Lord God with you. I pray that the Lord God Almighty will set an impenetrable wall around your mind and heart that no powers of darkness can breach. I pray that the Lord God will dispatch mighty angels on your behalf to set up camp around you right now and comfort you as you take a step toward walking in obedience to the One who loves you most.

To take this step, pray the following prayer:

> *Faithful Father, I confess that I have been holding on to unforgiveness in my heart. I come to You right now in humility, seeking Your grace and mercy. Lord God, I know that in Jesus, the Holy Spirit is right here comforting me. Please show me whom I need to forgive and help me forgive them.*

Go through the list of narcissists who have hurt you that you wrote down in chapter 1, and write down the ones you have not forgiven. Today is your day of freedom. Write down their names, their relationship to you, and how they hurt you.

Name	Relationship to you	How you were affected by their narcissism

After you review your list, pray the following prayer about each person you identify:

> *Father, I choose to forgive [name] for the hurt they have caused me. Please uproot every poisonous seed the enemy has planted in my heart through this person and purge it out of my heart from its root—whether seeds of rejection, condemnation, deception, lies, insults, teasing, slander, or gossip—and render them null and void. Father, thank You that I am who You say I am. I am no longer defined by the perpetrators in my life, as I have forgiven them. Father, I ask You to bless them and protect them from the attacks of the enemy. I pray they will draw close to You with all their heart, soul, mind, and strength and that You will be glorified in their lives. In Jesus' mighty name, amen.*

There are times when we forgive our perpetrators yet still feel a lingering hurt that hasn't subsided. This is an indication that you have inner vows connected to the wound. Inner vows are declarations we made to ourselves in times of pain, aiming to prevent future suffering. For example: "I'll never be like my mother." Inner vows can take the form of either verbal declarations or heart commitments we make to ourselves. Though they may seem harmless at the time, these inner vows act like contracts binding us to live up to the vow we made. The following are the four problems with inner vows.

Reactive

Vows are reactive in nature because they come from a place of pain, not a place of peace. As we've covered so far, the enemy intentionally puts a narcissist in your life to cause you pain because he knows this pain will make you vulnerable. Then he tempts you to make a vow based on the hurt you feel. Satan understands the power of our will and that we will strive to fulfill whatever promises we make to ourselves. Not only are inner vows driven by our own desires, but they are also influenced by the enemy's plan to harm us—the same enemy who seeks to steal, kill, and destroy us. (See John 10:10.)

Self-determining

Whether positive, such as, "I'll have the highest degree in the family," or negative, such as, "I'll never amount to anything," these inner vow statements are a form of self-idolatry in which we attempt to determine our own path. When we make inner vows, we're choosing our will over God's will, and unless they are repented of, we risk living out the vow we made.

The enemy is cunning. He knows how to whisper in our ears in a way that entices us to agree with his recommendations to self-protect. He knows that by placing ourselves under our own authority, we're acting in rebellion against God, who said in 1 Samuel 15:23, "For rebellion is like the sin of divination." In other words, opposing God's will by asserting our will is similar to heeding the instruction of evil spirits.

Judgmental stance

This one's a hard pill to swallow, but it's the truth. When we make inner vows, they are often made from a place of judgment. That's not to say the narcissist in your life is without fault; however, it goes back to putting yourself in God's position rather than leaving judgment to the rightful one. The apostle Paul wrote, "Do not take revenge, my dear friends, but leave room for God's wrath, for it is written: 'It is mine to avenge; I will repay,' says the Lord" (Rom. 12:19).

When you don't judge based on the leading of the Spirit, you leave yourself vulnerable to the enemy's deception. Imagine a woman who, because of her critical father, treats all men as if they were critical. She made a judgment call long ago, determining that this is how men are, and therefore treats them accordingly.

Binding

The Bible says, "Whoever sows to please their flesh, from the flesh will reap destruction; whoever sows to please the Spirit, from the Spirit will reap eternal life" (Gal. 6:8).

By making an inner vow, you're tying that person's behavior to your identity—even if the enemy has convinced you that you're actually separating yourself from that person. Even if you define yourself as the complete opposite of those who hurt you, you'll constantly strive to prove you're different. Thus, you're still confining yourself to a trajectory that stems from an unhealed wound.

Here is an example of how I've seen this play out. Let's say you're a mom who was raised by a narcissistic parent. Your parent was critical of you. It seemed that no matter what you did, it was never good enough. As you got older, you dreamed of the day you'd have children so you could love them the way you needed to be loved as a child.

The enemy knows this, so he turns the role of parenting, which was given to you by God, into a means by which you cover up an unhealed wound, and he convinces you to go about it by becoming the best parent you can be. Well, "What's wrong with that?" you might ask. The issue is you've made a decision based on pain and an unhealed wound.

Making a socially acceptable vow such as, "I'll be the best parent," might seem fine at first. But I've seen in counseling that it can have negative long-term effects. For example, moms who dedicate themselves to being the best mom base their definition of that on the opposite of what they received or didn't receive growing up. This opens the door for the enemy to whisper condemnation and guilt every time they fall short of their high expectations.

To fulfill the inner vow a mom made to herself, she ends up becoming so involved in giving her child everything she didn't have growing up that she loses herself in the process. The mom begins to see her child as a part of herself. One day when the child grows up and wants to leave, the mom feels lost and anxious. She may even resent the child for being ungrateful or wanting to leave. The reality is, this mom was unknowingly using her child to cover up her own wounds that she never dealt with. This is how the enemy takes advantage of unhealed wounds—by tempting you to make a vow that keeps you bound. For this mother, the way to move forward in this step is to forgive her mom, then deal with the inner vows that stemmed from her wounds.

The way to deal with a vow is to identify it, confess it, repent of it, and renounce it.

To identify which vows you have made, I encourage you to get with the Lord and pray the following prayer:

> *Lord Jesus, I confess that there have been many times in my life when I sought to do my own will rather than Your will. Whether this was done because I was afraid or through sheer rebellion, I come before You today as it says in Hebrews 4:16, to approach the throne of grace boldly, that I may receive grace and mercy in*

this time of need. Lord God, please examine my heart just as David prayed for you to do in Psalm 139:23–24, and as I go through the list of vows, please show me which vows I have made, whether consciously or subconsciously, so that I can repent of them and cut off their effects from my life. I want to live in the freedom You have granted me in Your Son, my Lord Jesus Christ. And Father, if there are any vows I have made that are not on this list, please bring them to mind too so I can confess them, repent of them, and renounce them. I pray this in the mighty name of Jesus. Amen.

Below is a list of common inner vows that stem from narcissistic abuse. I encourage you to go through this list of vows slowly and identify which ones resonate with you and either circle or highlight them. You've asked God to help you, and He is faithful. He will do it.

» I'll never get close to someone again.

» I'll never be known as a failure.

» I'll never let them get the best of me again.

» I'll never let anyone break my heart again.

» I'll never let anyone hurt me again.

» I'll never trust anyone again.

» I'll never cry in front of people again.

» I'll never let a man/woman see my emotions.
» I'll never let myself be vulnerable again.
» I will not let a man/woman control me.
» I'll never open my heart to anyone again.
» I'll never share my true feelings.
» I'll never get married.
» I'll never get close to a pastor again.
» I'll never get close to people at church again.
» I'll never get close to an older man/woman again.
» I'll never seek out a mentor again.
» I'll never work for a man/woman again.
» I'll never abandon my kids like ___________.
» I'll never listen to a preacher again.
» I'll never believe a preacher again.
» I'll never go to church again.
» I'll never take a leap of faith again.
» I'll never act like my _____________________.
» I'll always need support from my family.
» I'll never have a job that supports my lifestyle.
» I'll never let myself feel again.

» I'll never leave my children like my _________ left me.

» I'll never treat my children like my _________ treated me.

» I'll never preach the gospel.

» I'll always support my family.

» I'll always be a good mother/father.

» I'll never try to do that again.

» Other: ________________________________.

Once you're done identifying the vows you have made in the past, using each inner vow, pray the following prayer:

Lord Jesus, I confess vowing that ____________ ________________________. I renounce that vow, and in the name of Jesus, I uproot it from the root and cancel all its effects on me and my life.

Once you're done confessing and renouncing, pray:

Father, I repent of making those vows. Thank You that You are compassionate and full of mercy and grace. Lord, forgive me for stepping outside Your will, for putting myself in the judgment seat, and for pronouncing these vows on my life. I confess that I am not the god of my life. I confess that people are not the gods of my life. I confess that things are not the gods of my life.

Lord Jesus, I confess that You are the Lord of lords and King of kings, and you are the God of my life. Please forgive me for my ignorance in making these vows. I repent of self-righteousness and self-pity.

Father, in the mighty name of Jesus, I break each one of the vows I have confessed and I ask You to break any influence they've had over my life. I pray that You will heal the hurts in which these vows were rooted. Please realign my life according to Your will. Restore to me the joy of my salvation. Teach me to do Your will, for You are the God of my salvation. Into Your hands I entrust my life.

Once you've acted in obedience to God by forgiving your perpetrator and severed agreement with lies and inner vows, your next move is to step into the authority Christ has given you in Him. This last phase includes confessions and prayers of declaration to come into agreement with what God has already said is true. Now, these prayers are not magic formulas but rather a way to align your heart, mind, and spirit with God's Word. As you use whichever prayers resonate with you, do so with faith in the fact that Christ has already won your freedom, as John 8:36 says, "If the Son sets you free, you will be free indeed."

Conquering Self-Defeat

The path to overcoming the cycle of self-defeat begins with you acknowledging and confessing the doubt you've held on to in regards to God's willingness to protect you—and confessing having sought to meet your need to feel loved using measures outside of God. This is not something you're confessing to shame or condemn yourself but rather to be transparent and open your heart to God and exchange the methods you've been using with what He has for you, trusting that His way is better.

By denouncing the lies and repenting of them, you're calling them lies and purging them out of your heart, choosing to take hold of the truth instead. In that way, you open your eyes to see yourself as you truly are in Christ.

If you're ready to overcome the cycle of self-defeat, let the following prayer be a step of faith:

> *Father, I come to You today knowing that my value comes from You alone. Lord, I confess that through the years, I've held on to the words people have used to describe me—poisonous seeds the enemy has planted within my heart. And because I kept seeking love from those who rejected me over and over, I left myself open to enemy attacks.*
>
> *Lord, I confess that out of a deep-seated insecurity and a paralyzing fear of rejection,*

I have turned to other measures to feel loved. Please bring to mind any other activities I have taken part in that were self-destructive so I may confess them, repent of them, and cut off their influence from my life. (Wait for God to bring these to mind—for example, drinking to numb your feelings, partying, prostituting, or self-medicating.)

Then continue,

Father, I confess taking part in (activities). I ask that You forgive me for each one I have engaged in, as I know that when I confess my sins to You, You are faithful to forgive me and cleanse me from all unrighteousness.

Turn my eyes from worthless things and give me life through Your Word. Open my spiritual eyes that I may see the immense love You have for me. Help me elevate Your opinion of me above the opinion of man. Set my feet on You as my foundation. Purge my heart of anything that is not of You, anything I believe that is contrary to Your Word, and fill me with Your Word. Give me a hunger for Your Word. May Your Holy Spirit fill every crevice in my heart. Expose the enemy's lies and fill me with Your truth. May the Holy Spirit on the inside of me act as a fortress for my heart. Give me discernment beyond my years through the indwelling Holy Spirit.

Father, I confess my passivity toward You. I declare that You are worthy. You have all the honor and praise. Your opinion is the only one that matters; You are the holder of justice, and You are the pure definition of love. *As I draw closer to You, teach me to see You as You are, rather than through the blemished filter of my experiences with people. Open my eyes to see myself through Your eyes, and help me see situations, whether from the past, present, or future, from Your perspective. Incline my ears to Your voice and my heart to Your will and my feet to follow You step by step, knowing that You, my Father, who has called me by name, are faithful to guide me day by day. Thank You that in You I am free from the trap of self-defeat. I have the mind of Christ and the Spirit of the living God living on the inside of me.*

When the enemy tries to entice me back into this trap You have set me free from, I pray that You'll send confusion into his camp and cause his demons to go running in fear and never come back to me again. And if any of Satan's demons get close to me, I pray in the mighty name of Jesus that You will silence their voice, that their plan will be rendered null and void, and that You will turn their evil schemes for good to bring You glory. Amen.

Overcoming Rebellion

Ending the cycle of rebellion begins with acknowledging that you've been putting trust in your own ability to protect yourself while denying your need to feel loved. To do this, it's important that you repent of any form of self-trust and declare your trust in God alone. The second part is repenting of any form of self-deceit, perpetuated by your enemy, Satan, who once convinced you that if you act as if you don't need to be loved, you won't get hurt. His goal is to leave you stuck in a perpetual state of fear. You were too afraid of feeling rejected by those who have hurt you and others who could hurt you that it blinded you to God's willingness to accept you. It blinded you to His ability to heal your wounds and satisfy your yearning for love.

Once you repent of the lie that you don't need to be loved, you can receive the healing God has for you in Jesus and feel the tangible love of the Holy Spirit. Repentance is an act of humility that says, "God, I confess I need Your love," and it opens the door for you to experience and receive His grace (Jas. 4:6).

If you're ready to overcome the cycle of rebellion, let the following prayer be a step of faith:

Father, I confess that out of my deep hurt I chose to deny my need for love, and as a result I sought to meet my own needs as a way of covering my wound. Today I uncover my wound before You, trusting that You care for me. I confess and repent of seeking to do my will and rejecting Your authority and others' authority in my life. Forgive me for the decisions I made willingly and subconsciously out of a place of rebellion. Please forgive me for holding on to the pain more than I've held on to You. Forgive me for holding on to beliefs that are not of You and seeking to satisfy myself and quench my need for love that only You could ever satisfy.

Father, I humbly come to You right now—vulnerable, exposed, broken—and pray that by the power of Your Holy Spirit, You will infiltrate every broken piece the enemy has shattered in my heart and repair it to stand against future attacks he may send my way. I declare my full allegiance to You alone and put my full trust in You. I pray for Your grace to cover me in the coming days, months, and years; for Your Spirit to lead me; and for You to give me a heart that seeks after You. I confess now that deep down all I ever wanted was someone to love me, and I've been searching in all the wrong places. You sought me out. You who are worthy pursued me to show me just how much You love me.

Father, I speak 2 Timothy 1:7 over my life, "that you have not given me a spirit of fear, but of power and of love, and of a sound mind." In times when the enemy entices me to make a decision before I seek Your will, help me stop and remember that I am not on my own but have a Father who loves me beyond measure, who wants to guide me and is looking out for me. Father, I thank You for Your endless grace that You've shown me over and over in Jesus. Thank You for Your mercies that are new every morning and available to me. Father, thank You that in Christ, I don't have to fear condemnation, but I can come to You boldly to seek Your grace. Thank You that in Christ, I get to call You my Abba Father, the one I belong to for eternity. Thank You, Lord Jesus, for Your endless sacrifice on my behalf. Thank You for making me Yours. Now help me live in a way that glorifies You most. In the mighty name of Jesus, amen.

Ending Over-Accommodation

Overcoming the cycle of over-accommodating begins with surrendering your desire to be needed to the One who can meet every need. If you're ready to overcome the cycle of over-accommodating, let the following prayer be a step of faith. It's not a magic formula but a sincere declaration of your desire to align with God's truth, repent from what's held you back, and walk in the freedom Christ has already made available to you.

Father, I come to You today with a heavy heart and a weary soul. I confess that I have trusted in myself to avoid people rejecting me. Lord, I confess that I've spent so much time trying to accommodate people in my life, and sometimes even under the veil of doing work for You. Please forgive me for putting trust in myself rather than entrusting myself to You. Forgive me for the times I've confessed You as my Lord and Savior yet acted otherwise by seeking to please people rather than You.

Lord, forgive me even for the times I sought to earn Your love, whether consciously or unconsciously, through works rather than humbly understanding that there is nothing I could ever do to earn Your love. Lord, I confess that You alone are worthy of praise. You alone are worthy of honor. Open my heart to understand Your redemptive love. Open my spiritual eyes to see just how much You love me.

Father, when the enemy entices me to go back to earn my worth, please still my spirit and whisper Your loving-kindness into the depths of my soul and remind me that in Christ, You already have given me worth. Father, from this day forward, I pledge my allegiance to You alone. Guide me with Your loving-kindness. May Your voice be louder than the enemy's voice in my mind. Father, protect me from doubt that will try to derail me from Your perfect plan and perfect will for my life. Shield my heart from fear that will try to put me back into the trap You have set me free from.

Father, thank You that in Jesus, I am Your child and You call me Yours. You call me Your beloved. In You I am safe. In You I am protected, and because You are my Father, I have nothing to fear. Thank You, Lord God, for being committed to guiding me along the best plan for my life that You have chosen for me. Fill my heart with Your love, and draw me to Your Word that I may quench my thirst for love. For You are the well of living water; help me draw from You that I may never thirst (John 6:35).

Father, when I start feeling anxious, help me seek You first, keep my feet from slipping, and keep my eyes on You, the author and finisher of my faith. Open my spiritual eyes so that I may see each problem I face from Your perspective, the right perspective, and remind me of Your love for me that it may still my soul.

Breaking Ties with Arrogance

Overcoming the trap of arrogance starts with acknowledging that you have been living a lie. This lie falsely made you believe you don't need God because you are already great or because you can rely on yourself. However, these beliefs were just tactics from the enemy to keep you trapped in your current situation.

Though coming out of this trap is very difficult because it feeds into our sinful nature, it is not impossible (Matt. 19:26). Overcoming the trap of arrogance comes down to choice. You must choose to put God on the throne of your life and understand that that is His proper place. Also understand that you were never meant to be the final authority on your life, or other people's lives, and believing that lie is how you got into the trap. The enemy knew that after the fall we as human beings inherited a sinful nature that works against us and seeks to exalt its will above God's will. So he used your own sinful nature against you to keep you stuck in a trap of seeking the praises of others to feel good about yourself. To overcome this trap, you have to denounce the works of the flesh in your life to the point where you're partnering with God against your sinful nature. As you starve your flesh, you then make a decision to discover who God designed you to be before He called the world into existence.

If you're ready to overcome the cycle of arrogance, let the following prayer be a step of faith:

Father, I come to You in humility, acknowledging that You despise an arrogant spirit. Forgive me for the contempt I have shown You over the years. Forgive me for rejecting You, and please forgive me for my unbelief. I confess that Jesus Christ is the Lord of my life, and in Him I am Your child. Father, I denounce the works of darkness that have been at work in my life, keeping me blind to the reality of who You've called me to be. Forgive me for the hurt I have caused in relationships. Forgive me for listening to the lies of the enemy and for following after his will for my life rather than Your will. Forgive me for following after my desires rather than Your desires. Thank You for the grace and mercy You have shown me through the years, as I know that Your kindness was meant to lead me to repentance that I may not perish. Thank You, Father, for the way You love me. Thank You, Lord Jesus, for dying on the cross for a wretched person like me that I may, through You, be counted as worthy.

Lord, I confess that I bring nothing to the table and You are the author of my faith, the Redeemer of my soul, my God, my fortress, the One who breathed life into me. Father, in the coming days, weeks, and months, I pray in the mighty name of Jesus that You'd instill an obedient spirit in me that follows Your lead. When the enemy whispers deceit in an attempt to derail me from Your will, I pray that You would silence his voice and turn my boldness, which the enemy has exploited against me, and use it against him that I may stand and declare as Paul did in Philippians 3:10, "I want to know Christ and experience the mighty power that raised him from the dead."

Father, give me a hunger for Your Word, and fill me with Your truth. Give me a heart that is teachable and receptive to Your correction, as I know that Your correction is affirmation of Your love. May my life glorify You. May people who knew the old me and watch the transformation You do in my heart stand in awe of You. Set a guard over my mouth, O Lord, and keep watch over the door of my lips. Let me not take a step ahead of You. May I follow You wherever You lead me. May my life serve as proof and a testimony to those who do not know You that You, Lord Jesus, are the King of kings, the Lord of lords, the mighty One who saves with His powerful, outstretched arm. Who can compare to You, Jehovah-Gibbor Milchamah ("the Lord mighty in battle"). *Thank You, Lord God, that though I didn't deserve it, You sought after me. You alone saved me, and You have made me new. May my life glorify You in every way. In Jesus' mighty name, amen.*

Chapter 10

DISMANTLING DREAD

THROUGHOUT THE PREVIOUS four chapters, we covered steps we must take to remove the enemy's footholds in our lives that made us vulnerable to narcissistic abuse. The process began with identifying the trap you're in so you would know not only how you got there but also how to overcome it. Then you moved forward to exchanging deceit with truth by surrendering yourself to the Lord Jesus Christ.

After this we exchanged doubt by renouncing lies we believed about God that the enemy has used to keep us from drawing close to God. We also renounced our allegiance to idols, with faith, by declaring our allegiance to God and entrusting ourselves to Him alone. In the last step, we exchanged disobedience for a life that is obedient to the Father by identifying unhealed wounds, forgiving our trespassers, renouncing inner vows we made from a place of hurt, and overcoming the specific trap(s) we identified with.

Now that you've completed intense inner work, there are two last steps that are make-or-break precautions to protect you from future narcissistic abuse. Without completing these steps, many people fall back into the arms of the abuser. These last two steps are more like principles we have to keep at the forefront of our minds to be able to spot narcissistic abuse from a mile away and stop it before it even begins.

Because these last two steps act as a protective measure that keeps you from falling back into the narcissist's traps, they must be exercised continually. That's why I refer to them as principles. We will cover one in this chapter and the other in the chapter that follows.

Principle 1: Fearing the Lord

In search of what makes the difference between someone who lives in a state of constant fear, anxiety, or depression and someone who doesn't, I found that the first determining factor lies in whether that person holds God in absolute reverence above anyone and everything else.

Reverence is often referred to in the Bible as *fearing the Lord*. Before we jump into the importance of this principle, I want to clarify that fear in connection with God does *not* mean being afraid of God in the sense that He will hurt you as His child. That's what dread is. Rather, it means you recognize that God's sovereignty is unmatched, and you live by the fact that God is all-powerful and holy and the One worthy of your reverence.

"So what does fearing the Lord have to do with my mental well-being?" you might ask. Let me explain: God made you with hormones that run through your body. These hormones have the capacity to either balance your mental state or wreak havoc on it. Your hormones are organized into three tiers of hierarchy. The hormones in tier 1 are the most important hormones in your body. If disrupted, they can throw off your entire system, causing you anxiety, fear, dread, and so forth.

As you see from the diagram on page 144, tier 1 hormones include cortisol (stress hormone), oxytocin (love hormone), and insulin (energy hormone).

Let's say you're facing a stressful situation. If you're facing it while stuck in one of the traps we talked about, you will likely either try to resolve it on your own or rely on people to resolve it. Either extreme puts you in a state where you're out of control. Even the illusion of control, such as when you try to resolve something on your own, still puts enough strain on your well-being that you feel stressed.

When you're under stress, your body releases a stress hormone called cortisol. This affects your oxytocin levels (your love hormone, responsible for helping you remain calm). Prolonged stress also affects your level of insulin, which regulates sugar in your body, causing it to become dysregulated. When tier 1 hormones are dysregulated, they throw tier 2 and tier 3 hormones out of balance, including those that can affect how you feel, such as melatonin (the sleep hormone). Now you're having trouble sleeping. That's why insomnia is one of the symptoms of anxiety and stress.

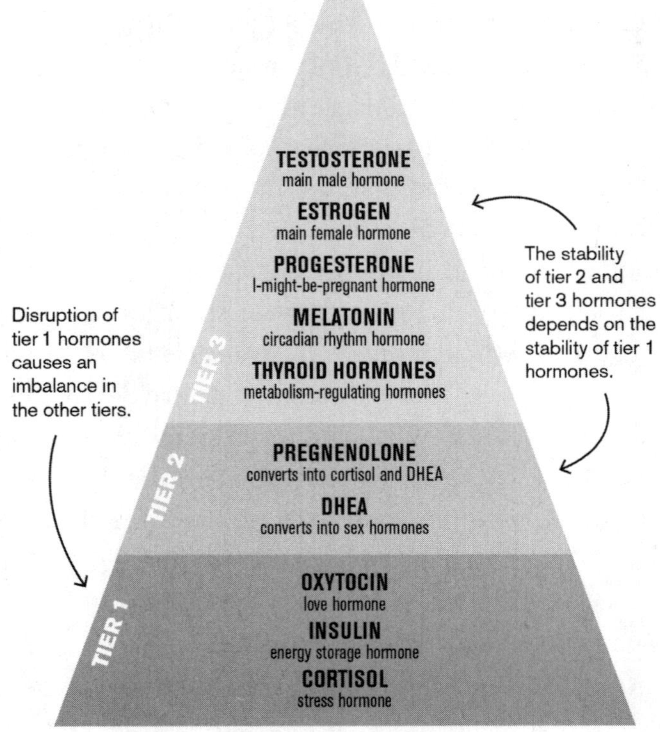

Using each trap God has set you free from, let's explore how fearing the Lord serves as a safeguard from future narcissistic abuse.

Arrogance

Avoiding this trap is not only about changing behavior. Similar to Saul's transformation into Paul or Jacob's transformation into Israel, a complete identity change is required. The purpose of God changing their name was to represent their change in identity.

The best way to make sure you don't fall back into the trap of arrogance is to watch your thoughts. Don't ever think the enemy will cease to whisper lies such as, "Do you really need God's permission for that too?" Don't ever think you've graduated to a certain level where you don't need God every single day of your life.

When God put me in a leadership position, He gave me a verse I've kept taped on my wall as a reminder not to become conceited.

> Brothers and sisters, think of what you were when you were called. Not many of you were wise by human standards; not many were influential; not many were of noble birth. But God chose the foolish things of the world to shame the wise; God chose the weak things of the world to shame the strong. God chose the lowly things of this world and the despised things—and the things that are not—to nullify the things that are, so that no one may boast before him. It is because of him that you are in Christ Jesus, who has become for us wisdom from God—that is, our righteousness, holiness and redemption.
>
> —1 Corinthians 1:26–30

Even with this verse on my wall, the enemy still takes every opportunity to get me to step out of God's will. To help keep yourself from becoming conceited, it's so important that you spend time with God every single day and submit to Him every decision you make, no matter how small or big. Don't let the enemy convince you that the decision is not big enough for you to run by God. Part of training yourself to submit to God is turning every decision over to Him. You're reminding yourself that you do answer to someone greater than you, and that person is the Lord God Almighty.

Your enemy hates it when you submit to God, because he knows that by doing so, you're closing the door for him to access that area of your life. Every area you submit to God is an area off-limits to the devil and his demons. They can try knocking, but if you've determined to submit it to God, they won't be able to influence it.

Rebellion

Resisting this trap requires you to make a conscious choice to submit your decisions to God's will. If you're prone to this trap, you're likely pretty decisive because you've gotten into the habit of figuring out your own way. It may be difficult at first, but remind yourself daily that you belong to God, who loves you unconditionally. As you entrust yourself to God, you see that He is different from the narcissist(s) you experienced. You'll begin to see how gentle and patient God truly is. And when you fall and genuinely repent, you'll realize just how forgiving your Father is.

Psalm 103:11–17 (NLT) says,

> For his unfailing love toward those who fear him is as great as the height of the heavens above the earth. He has removed our sins as far from us as the east is from the west. The LORD is like a father to his children, tender and compassionate to those who fear him. For he knows how weak we are; he remembers we are only dust. Our days on earth are like grass; like wildflowers, we bloom and die. The wind blows, and we are gone—as though we had never been here. But the love of the LORD remains forever with those who fear him.

As you include Your Father in your life, little by little you'll realize how much He has your best interest at heart. One day you'll be able to look back on decisions He guided you through that may not have made sense at the time, but when you look back, you'll realize just how much He was looking out for you. The more you realize that, the more determined you'll be not to let anything or anyone take precedence over your relationship with your heavenly Father.

Over-accommodating

Avoiding the trap of over-accommodating doesn't so much come down to whether you fear the Lord but whether you choose to fear the Lord *only*. Steering clear of this trap will require you to avoid distributing loyalties among those you perceive as your source of security, which gives the enemy opportunity to present people in your life to split your allegiance. To stay ahead of the enemy's tactic, routinely ask God to search your life and expose any areas where you prioritize someone or something over Him.

Remember that giving honor and giving allegiance are two totally different things. Giving honor to someone is pointing out their inherent dignity as an image bearer of God. This is what we're called to do: honor our parents and honor one another. You don't have to agree with someone to treat them with honor. Allegiance, however, signifies who and what you're willing to follow, who and what you're pledging your life to. If you tend to overaccommodate, be wary of the enemy giving you a divisive mind. This is a revolving door he uses to keep you stuck in a destructive pattern. You can profess Christ and go to church, but if you're not careful, the enemy can still deceive you into believing you need to keep certain people or things in your back pocket just in case God doesn't come through for you. Before you know it, you become a slave to all these people or things you have pledged your life to. The very people or things we use as our sources of safety become a snare to us (Ps. 106:36).

Whenever you feel pulled in a certain direction, before you take a step toward it, pause and ask if God is really prompting you to take that step or whether you're trying to accommodate because you've gotten into the habit of wanting that person or thing to give you an inner sense of peace. That's why praying Psalm 139:23–24 is so important. Ask Him to search you and point out what needs to be changed. Through a relationship with Him you'll see for yourself that His yoke is easy and His burden is light (Matt. 11:28–30). You'll also see that in Jesus, God has already lifted the burden for you, and in Him, whatever God has commissioned you to do, He will enable you to do by His Holy Spirit. Your part is to trust Him.

Self-defeat

Steering clear of this trap doesn't have as much to do with whether you fear God but whether you hold an unhealthy fear of God *along with* an enhanced fear of man. To live out the principle of fearing God alone will require you to fight against lies the enemy throws your way about God. If you've identified a propensity toward this trap, go back through the list of lies we went over in chapter 6 from time to time. Make sure you stay in the Word.

There have been times in my life when the enemy's attack was so hard I opened my Bible and started reading the Word out loud. Demons hate the Word. It makes them tremble. It exposes their lies, and it reminds them of just how weak they are in the presence of God. When you read the Word out loud, you're speaking God's truth, and the enemy—the father of lies—hates that because by receiving the truth of God's Word, you're undoing the very lies he's sewn into your heart.

Regardless of which trap you lean toward, remember, your enemy does not want you to spend time with God. Watch out for distractions he brings your way, whether it's your phone or someone who calls you about something right before you start spending time with God. I encourage you to put your phone away and set that time aside to feast on the Word. As you do and you learn more and more about God's character, you'll see not only just how powerful He is but also how merciful He is and how He offers you that mercy each and every day. You'll also see that He is for you. All you have to do is trust that He is and call on Him. Ask Him to teach you as David did in Psalm 86:11–13:

> Teach me your way, Lord, that I may rely on your faithfulness; give me an undivided heart, that I may fear your name. I will praise you, Lord my God, with all my heart; I will glorify your name forever. For great is your love toward me; you have delivered me from the depths, from the realm of the dead.

In Jesus, God has already won the biggest battle of your life—the battle of your soul. If He was sovereign enough to snatch you out of the enemy's grip, don't you think He's greater than all the demons combined? Your job is to believe that though God is sovereign, He's merciful to you and wants to be involved in the details of your life. He wants to lead you and show you whether to go left or right, because He loves you, and He cares enough to want to protect you.

I don't know what your childhood was like, but I can tell you this: Your Father is able to redeem everything the enemy has taken from you. You may not be able to redo the past, but if you trust Him, your present and your future will speak of the glory of God. Trust Him and include Him in the details of your life. Before you take a step, ask Him if this is from Him or not from Him. Ask Him to quicken your spirit if something is not from Him, and watch how at peace you will be knowing you're in the very will of the sovereign Lord of the universe. When you experience walking with God, you won't exchange the rest you feel—knowing you're in His will and protection—for anything the devil presents to you as a substitute.

Walking in the Fear of God

Fearing the Lord means choosing to never put anything or anyone above God in your life. Fearing the Lord also comes with the humility of knowing you have an enemy who is very dangerous and that this enemy will never stop presenting opportunities or putting people in your life to derail you from your relationship with God. And so part of fearing the Lord means stopping to ask yourself, "Is this something God wants me to do, or is this something I want to do and I'm asking God to bless it?" That, my friend, is the difference between asserting your will and getting back on the enemy's track for your life, and asserting God's will for your life, knowing He knows what is best for you.

Fearing the Lord means caring more about what God wants than what we want. That's what it means to crucify our flesh. Sometimes it's very obvious, and other times it's not. Years ago my friend gave birth to her baby and experienced complications during the delivery. Thankfully, she and her baby were OK. Throughout my friend's recovery I felt I needed to be there with her. Little by little I began to spend more time with her. One night while having dinner with my husband, I told him I would need to watch church with my friend the next day while I helped her. In other words, he'd have to go to church with our children, without me. My husband objected. I couldn't believe he did, so I immediately rebutted his objection by reminding him that God tells us to visit people in hospitals and to care for the sick.

Jeremiah 17:9 says, "The heart is deceitful above all things." We can deceive ourselves into believing we're in the right—that is, until we invite God into the situation and humbly ask Him to give us His perspective. That night after dinner I talked to God about the situation. I asked Him what He thought. Immediately the Lord showed me the point at which helping my friend stopped being about serving Him and became about me feeling important to my friend. If you want to distinguish whether you're truly doing something for Him or doing it for you, ask yourself, "If I overheard the person I helped acknowledge someone else who helped them but didn't acknowledge me, would I feel upset?"

For me the answer to that question would have been, "Yes, I'd be upset." I repented of derailing from God's will during that time. The Lord reminded me graciously that He owns my time and that when He wants me to help someone, He will move my heart to help them and there will be no ulterior motive behind it. One time a friend told me about a friend of hers who was moving to an apartment and had nothing. The Lord moved in my heart ever so strongly to help this person get set up in their apartment. There was no ulterior motive behind it. I barely knew this person, so there would've been no reason for me to help them, apart from God ordaining it that way. That is the difference between a Spirit-led step and a flesh-enticed step.

Fearing the Lord also means getting in the habit of asking yourself, "What do I fear the most?" Is it not being liked? Is it not being included? Sure, being liked and included may feel good, but if we are driven by them, they'll drive us right into the arms of a narcissist and result in one of the traps we talked about in the earlier chapters.

On the other hand, if we fear breaking our Father's heart because we love and respect Him, we'll ask Him to be in every detail of our lives so as not to misstep. Does this mean you'll never misstep? Obviously not, but when you do, God will gently tug at your heart to bring you back in line with His will.

The Bible compares Satan to a roaring lion seeking someone to devour. Your enemy is never going to stop looking for an opportunity to make you fall. The fear of the Lord, however, will serve as a shield in your life to keep you from falling for enemy tactics.

The Book of 1 Corinthians was written to a group of believers. It says, "If you think you are standing firm, be careful that you don't fall!" (10:12). Here, Paul is reminding us to stay vigilant, recognizing that we are in a spiritual war in which the enemy of our souls desires nothing more than to devour us. Paul continues with this reassurance, showing what the enemy uses to get us to fall: "No temptation has overtaken you except what is common to mankind. And God is faithful; he will not let you be tempted beyond what you can bear. But when you are tempted, he will also provide a way out so that you can endure it" (vv. 13–14).

Regarding the friend I helped at the hospital, I know the exact point at which it stopped being about God and became about me. Paul continues: "Therefore, my dear friends, flee from idolatry" (v. 15).

God is faithful. If you seek His face and ask Him to protect you from temptation, I believe He will give you checks in your spirit. Through the years, recognizing how cunning the enemy is, my prayer has become:

> *Father, please keep me from stepping outside Your will, whether knowingly or unknowingly. If I make one step outside Your will, Lord, convict me and get my attention. I want nothing more than You in my life. I love You, Lord. In Jesus' name.*

I encourage you to make this prayer part of your daily life and mean it. Seek His face and His presence. May the fear of the Lord, your God and Father, shield you from temptation the enemy presents to you.

In the next chapter we'll look at principle 2, part of the make-it-or-break-it precautions that determine whether you live a life of just muddling along or a life of victory!

Chapter 11

CLAIMING VICTORY

BEFORE THE LORD called me into the field of counseling, I worked in sales. Part of selling a product required identifying an existing problem in the potential customer's life and helping them with a solution. As with everything, the enemy has warped this method to exploit us. In the garden he approached Eve and deceived her into believing she had a problem that, oh, by the way, didn't even exist, then offered her a solution!

Thousands of years later he continues to play the same game in our lives. He strategically places a narcissist in our lives to distort how we see ourselves and those in authority over us, with a specific emphasis on God. He manipulated us into accepting false beliefs about God we went over in earlier chapters. Once we took the bait, he introduced a substitute we would accept.

In chapter 2 we covered some of the story of Jacob and Esau from Jacob's perspective, who, based on the clinical criteria for narcissism, once fit the bill. Now let's look at the same story from Esau's standpoint to show you how he fell for Jacob's trick. This will show you how to discern when a narcissist is trying to exploit you.

Genesis 25:24–26 recalls:

> When the time came for her [Rebecca] to give birth, there were twin boys in her womb. The first to come out was red, and his whole body was like a hairy garment; so they named him Esau. After this, his brother came out, with his hand grasping Esau's heel; so he was named Jacob. Isaac was sixty years old when Rebekah gave birth to them.

So, as you see, Esau was the rightful recipient of the birthright, which was an honorary position that gave a firstborn the right to receive a double portion of his father's inheritance. When the brothers were older, Genesis 25:29–36 says,

> Once when Jacob was cooking some stew, Esau came in from the open country, famished. He said to Jacob, "Quick, let me have some of that red stew! I'm famished!" (That is why he was also called Edom.) Jacob replied, "First sell me your birthright." "Look, I am about to die," Esau said. "What good is the birthright to me?" But Jacob said, "Swear to me first." So he swore an oath to him, selling his birthright to Jacob. Then Jacob

> gave Esau some bread and some lentil stew. He ate and drank, and then got up and left.

It's clear from this exchange that Esau didn't value his birthright so as to exchange it for a bowl of stew. And that leads us to principle 2, the last of the two steps that will help you remain rooted in the freedom you've already begun to experience.

Principle 2: Walking in Your Birthright

Centuries later the enemy has banked on us having the same ignorance Esau did so as not to value the birthright we have in Christ. Since you are in Christ, when you were born again, you inherited the birthright status. But if you don't take hold of who you are in Christ by spending time with God and letting Him fill the void this fallen world left you with, when the enemy comes in to whisper lies, you won't have truth in you to compare the lies with. So you'll end up being deceived and accept whatever he offers you. That's the majority of the reason we fall for narcissistic abuse.

If, however, you let God fill your void by reading His Word, spending time with Him, and letting Him tell you who you are, when the enemy comes in with his whispers, the Holy Spirit will bring to mind the truth that has been planted in you through the Word you've been feeding on, and as a result, you'll reject the enemy's lies.

As a counselor, I study patterns of behavior and try to link those patterns to a root. In doing so, I can tell you with full assurance that the reason the enemy is able to derail us back into one of the four traps we went over is that we don't know how much God truly loves us, and as a result, we don't invest the time to get to know who we are in Him.

Listen, your enemy is after your identity because he knows that who you believe you are determines your behavior and essentially plays a crucial role in transforming a life of defeat into a life of victory, regardless of what's happening externally.

The reason so many children of God still live defeated is that they have not yet taken hold of their birthright status that was given to them when they gave their life to Jesus.

In the counseling room I come across so many patients who profess Jesus as their Lord and Savior, go to church, and may even be in ministry, but they still see themselves as sinners who are trying their best rather than as children of God, loved by their Father, who are going through the sanctification process. And trust me, there's a difference! If deep down you believe you are a sinner who is trying to do good things to keep God happy, then you're putting yourself back under the yoke of the law rather than living under the grace Jesus provided on your behalf.

The law is where the enemy wants you to live because he knows that as long as you see yourself as a sinner who's trying their best, it's only a matter of time before you get frustrated with yourself, frustrated with God, and frustrated with others, and give up on ever being loved by God, as in the trap of *self-defeat*. Why? Because you've put the burden of being lovable on yourself to achieve and maintain. Or you may give in and live overwhelmed and resentful of those you are serving to gain their love, as in the trap of *over-accommodating.* Or you may commit to looking out for yourself, as in the trap of *rebellion.* All these scenarios stem from the same thing: You do not (yet) honor your birthright as a son or daughter of God—like Esau, who did not put value on his birthright, and the Israelites, who kept getting plundered and falling over and over.

The reason the enemy can successfully introduce one narcissist after another into our lives, or at least use one situation after another, is that we hold no value on ourselves as children of God. This is why I made it a huge point to start out the two principles with *fear of the Lord* first and then *walking in your birthright.* If you don't respect the One you belong to, you'll never respect yourself.

Throughout the next few pages, using each trap, we're going to identify the barriers that keep us from walking in our birthright and how to overcome our barriers so we can exchange defeat for a life marked by victory.

Arrogance

To stay out of this trap, understand that although you were born as an image bearer of God, your worth flows from your identity as a child of God, and your submission to Him reflects your trust in that relationship.

As I was writing this, the Lord gave me an image of an ironing tool. You can't effectively use an iron without it being plugged in. No matter how nice it is, if it's not plugged in, it cannot function the way it's intended. I wondered why God didn't give me an image of something else that can work independently rather than a tool that needs not only a plug but an ironing board as well to work effectively. As I sought the Lord, He showed me how someone who has the propensity toward this trap needs to understand that they can only draw their source from God, but they also need to understand their need for people (the ironing board).

Can you iron without an ironing board? Sure, I've done it when I was in a rush, but it didn't come out as well as if I had ironed my clothes properly. And if I had the iron, the ironing board would be useless if I didn't also have an electrical outlet. So just remember that while you are an image bearer of God, your identity and your purpose are directly attached to the One who made you. You can try to use people as your source of praise so you feel worthy as much as you want, but it's just as if you were trying to iron something on an ironing board with a cold iron. It would only lead to frustration. Instead, experience the joy of not having to strive for your worth by submitting to the One who loves you most and drawing your worth from Him.

Let's say you've submitted your life to Christ. How do you practically resist the enemy's future deception and attempts to get you back into the trap of arrogance?

1. Identify your weak points, and understand where the enemy took hold of you to begin with.

One way he got you to fall into the trap of arrogance was by putting someone in your life who overflattered you and convinced you that you are valuable independent of God. So Satan may try to get you back into this cycle by placing somebody in your life who will overflatter you and stroke your ego to steer you away from drawing your value from God.

If you're reading or listening to this and God brings someone to mind who's doing this to you, repent of entertaining flattery, and ask Him to forgive you and help you stay vigilant because even when you resist this person, Satan is relentless. You can be sure he will present another opportunity. That's why it's so important that you repair the root by shifting the source you drew your value from. Once you determine that you're drawing your value from God *alone*, you'll be unresponsive to the people the enemy uses to stroke your ego or opportunities he presents that offer you admirable success.

2. Whenever an opportunity presents itself, ask, "Is this from You, Lord?"—and wait for Him to respond.

God is faithful. Get to know how He talks to you. For some, He confirms His direction through dreams. For others, He gives His peace to move forward or a check in their spirit to keep them from moving forward toward an opportunity. Ask God to show you how He leads you. God's voice will never contradict His Word. When you ask Him, He is faithful to show you.

3. If the enemy can't get you to step out of God's will, he will put someone in your life who will be a source of grief to you.

This person will try their best to outshine you so they can get you to kick your flesh back into gear to try to compete with them for attention, for admiration, or to flat-out prove yourself worthy. Resist the attempt and see it for what it is. This is merely your enemy grabbing at straws because he knows that without you accepting his deception as truth, and without you volunteering to step out of God's will, he is powerless.

Over-accommodating

To stay out of this trap, keep in mind that while relationships with others are important, your relationship with God must be first. That doesn't mean just attending church or doing missionary work. It means making time to have dates with your heavenly Father. There may be times when you feel unworthy or doubt if God is really spending time with you. Recognize this as a lie from the enemy. Don't listen to him. Better yet, when you recognize this attack, read God's Word out loud to yourself. God's Word isn't the same as therapeutic affirmations. God's Word is alive and active because it's absolute truth (Heb. 4:12). Therefore, the Word has the capacity to pierce through lies the enemy has planted in your heart, expose them, and uproot them.

God's Word is an offensive weapon against the powers of darkness. So when your enemy says, "Why would you think God wants to spend time with you? Who do you think you are?" speak the Word by saying something like, "Father, thank You for the way You love me. Thank You for this time I get to spend with You."

One of the biggest hurdles to staying out of this trap is a question I've heard from patients: "Why did God choose me?" People ask this question to try to qualify themselves. If you feel unworthy of God choosing you, you try to qualify why He didn't. The reality is that none of us was worthy of God choosing us. God alone is worthy, and in His love He decided to be merciful to us, as He says in Exodus 33:19, "I will cause all my goodness to pass in front of you, and I will proclaim my name, the Lord, in your presence. I will have mercy on whom I will have mercy, and I will have compassion on whom I will have compassion."

Although there's nothing you ever could have done to earn God wanting a relationship with you, He decided to make you His child to love you. And when you gave your life to Jesus, He sealed you with the Holy Spirit, marking you as His. So to resist going back into the trap of over-accommodating, get in the habit of spending time with God, and don't stop there. Talk to Him throughout the day; include Him in your day-to-day decisions. The reason you got into this trap is that you value relationships, and although you were made for connection and relationship, your foundational relationship has to be with God first. It feeds all your other relationships. Out of your relationship with God, you're able to have healthy connections and relationships with other people, but your source must always be God.

Your enemy is never going to stop presenting you with opportunities and people who need you, because he knows that's how he can derail you back into the trap of over-accommodating. It's a slow fade that starts with one step in the wrong direction. But if you are determined to let the fear of God lead you because you value Him and value your relationship with Him, you will be able to discern whether something is from God or is a derailment from the enemy because you won't take a step without your Father's say-so.

Even in times when you start heading in the wrong direction, God is faithful to alert you to get back on track with His will. On Mondays I dedicate the first couple of hours of the day to reading the Word. At the time, since I was only treating patients a couple of days a week, I decided to add on a couple more on Monday, during the time I usually spend with God. As soon as I set out in my heart to do so, I started having nightmares that I was unfaithful to my husband. The first two times I had dreams like this, I was very disturbed.

Through the years, I've learned that God uses this type of dream to alert me that I am choosing something or someone over Him. After the third night of having this dream, I sought the Lord, and the answer was clear that I was about to replace my time with Him with something else. So I canceled my plan to take on more patients. The nightmares ceased.

I'm sharing this to show you that only God can satisfy the connection you so deeply crave, the connection that is in all our hearts, regardless of which trap we fall into.

God also cares about the details of your life. God longs for your time and devotion because He is protective over you and knows how easy it is for the enemy to sway you.

When you value God, you'll also value your time with Him—and your Father will lovingly correct you when the enemy does try to derail you. All you have to do is respond in obedience and get back on track. So again, if this trap resonates with you, make sure you do the following:

» Spend time reading the Word. Write down key scriptures and repeat them to yourself so that when the enemy attacks you with thoughts that make you doubt whether God wants to spend time with you, you can quickly recognize them as false. Spiritual warfare starts with deception, the opposite of truth. The Word is truth. Your main weapon against thoughts that lead to anxiety is speaking the Word out loud to yourself.

» Watch out for enemy-enticed opportunities. The enemy knows how to get you to kick your flesh into gear by placing someone in your life who needs you because he knows that if he can get you roped in, you'll start drawing your need to feel valued from that person rather than from the true source—God.

Suppose you're talking to a friend who expresses a need to you. Before rushing in to help your friend, pause and ask God, "Is this something You want me to do?"

I know we are called to be the hands and feet of Jesus. I'm not arguing that; what I am saying, however, is that before you take a step toward something that looks like a good opportunity, pray something like, "Lord, _______________ seems to need XYZ, and I feel a pull to meet this need for them. Please show me whether this is something You want me to do. If so, give me peace about it. If this isn't something You want me to act on, I ask that You will quicken my spirit to discern that it's not Your will. Father, please teach me to do Your will. And protect me from the enemy. Amen."

James 1:5–6 says, "If any of you lacks wisdom, you should ask God, who gives generously to all without finding fault, and it will be given to you. But when you ask, you must believe and not doubt, because the one who doubts is like a wave of the sea, blown and tossed by the wind." When you ask your Father for wisdom, He is faithful to lead you. When He shows you, don't overthink it. Take what God tells you and keep moving forward.

Rebellion

To steer clear of this trap, you have to resist the enemy's temptation to self-validate your worth through your own efforts. Understand that your worth is not yours to give but rather something you have to look to God for. Now, this thought may be scary because you may feel as if you're putting yourself at the mercy of someone who is holy—and therefore has even more reason to reject you.

When this thought comes to mind, resist it and identify it as the enemy trying to derail you back into this trap. Remember, God had every reason to reject you. The Bible shows that while we were still sinners, God sent Jesus to die on the cross for us so we would have a chance to have a relationship with Him. The Bible also shows that our worth has been established by God.

A year or so before I gave my life to Jesus, the Lord sent me a series of dreams in which I was washing blood off a toddler's hands and feet. Years later I came across Ezekiel 16:9, which says, "I bathed you with water and washed the blood from you and put ointments on you." In this passage the Lord was reminding the Israelites who had rebelled against Him that their worth didn't come from themselves; rather, it came from Him.

Similarly, just as God showed me in my dream when I was trapped in rebellion, He is the One who accepts us and then cleans us up. Grasping this truth and believing it are key in putting an end to the constant need to prove your worth to yourself and others to the point of exhaustion, only to wake up the next day and have to do it again. Remaining out of this trap requires that you do the following:

» Push past the lie that you can achieve your own worth and get off the bandwagon of having to prove it. Understand that you took that stance out of fear of rejection. But, just as God showed me in my dream, He does not accept us as children of God because we get things right. Rather, He pursued us in our sinful nature that had made us undeserving of His acceptance and through Jesus offered us a parent-child relationship, where He accepted us and now transforms us by His Spirit.

» Realize that God will convict you for the purpose of protecting you from falling back into this cycle. God's accepting you fully does not mean He's going to condone a sinful lifestyle. So when you sin, resist the temptation to shut down and run away from God, and also resist listening to the enemy's condemnation. Condemnation is part of Satan's trick; he tempts you, and then he condemns you so you will run away from God. That's what he did with Adam and Eve. This is so important: When you sin and feel convicted, run to your Father (Heb. 4:16), confess your sin to Him (1 John 1:9), and believe that the One who called you has not given up on you.

Self-defeat

To keep yourself from falling back into this trap, understand that those who treated you as unworthy didn't have the capacity to set your worth to begin with. Years ago I overheard two children arguing. One child told the other, "You're bad!" The other child responded by crying, running to his parent, and saying, "I'm bad." When the parent asked why he thought that, the child responded, "Milly [name changed] called me bad." The parent answered ever so gently, "Milly doesn't have the authority to decide whether you're bad; only God does, and He calls you very good."

Similarly, the people Satan used to hurt you and sow lies in your heart didn't create you and therefore didn't have the capacity to dictate whether you're worthy. Even if the people who hurt you were authority figures over you, their God-given authority extended only to the purpose of guiding you and protecting you, not dictating your worth. The only one who can speak to your worth is the One who made you.

Truth is truth, whether we believe it or not. Your Father has already declared you as a child of God worthy. On a daily basis you have to choose whether you're going to believe Him or listen to people who don't have the authority to call out your worth. To make sure you walk this out, I encourage you to do the following two things:

» Get in the habit of spending time with God.

In my early years of walking with God, after I had gotten over the hump of running from God whenever I sinned, I finally realized He wasn't going to strike me down when I went to Him and sought forgiveness. Throughout my relationship with God, He has shown me a significant correlation: Whenever I neglected spending time with Him or failed to prioritize my time with Him, I started seeking and drawing validation and worth from other avenues.

It does not matter how long you walk with the Lord; you never get to a point where you are so full you don't need Him anymore. This is like trying to feed off one meal per week—and depending on that one meal to sustain you the rest of the week. You'd end up sick and most likely craving anything and everything you smelled.

You and I were made to be dependent on God, where He guides us each day. The incredible thing is that God willingly does it. All you have to do is seek Him and ask Him to guide you. Get in His Word. Close your social media app that reminds you of what you're missing, and open your Bible so He can remind you of who you are in Him. When you dedicate intentional time to spend with your Father, you'll realize that in Him you have the best of the best. He made you, so He knows how to fill you in a way that you are so satisfied that when the devil uses one of his demons to whisper thoughts of condemnation to you, you'll be able to discern, "These are not my thoughts," and start thanking God for the way He loves you. Remember, praise is a mighty weapon!

» Ask the Lord to help you recognize His voice versus the enemy's voice.

This is one of the biggest hurdles you will have to overcome, especially if you have the propensity toward the trap of self-defeat. God is the ultimate authority of your life, and therefore in Christ any condemning and accusatory thoughts and words that were spoken to you are *void*. Why? Because those people didn't have the authority to speak those words over you, nor do you have the authority to speak them yourself because you are not your own (1 Cor. 6:19–20); you were bought with the price of the shed blood of Jesus Christ.

Keep in mind that demons often whisper condemning/accusatory thoughts in the first person (meaning, it sounds like your own thoughts) because they know we're more likely to entertain them if we mistake them for our own thoughts. Once the thought hits your mind, your job as a steward of God's temple, which includes your brain and heart, is to discern whether that thought is congruent with who God says you are. If it is not, you are to cast it down (2 Cor. 10:5) by speaking God's truth to yourself, about yourself.

The following chart includes the most common condemning/accusatory thoughts Satan plants in our minds, in the first person, in hopes that we will receive them and allow them into our hearts. This chart serves as a way for you to guard your heart as Proverbs 4:23 instructs us to do. You can use the following examples regardless of which trap you lean toward.

Reversing Demonic Thoughts with the Truth
I'm a loser. ⇨⇨ Father, thank You for calling me Your child.
I'll never make a comeback from this. ⇨⇨ Thank You, Lord, that with You nothing is impossible!
I'm a disappointment. ⇨⇨ Thank You, Lord, that though I had nothing to offer You, You sought me out, You made me Yours, and You delight in me.
I'll never be like my ____________. ⇨⇨ Father, I thank You that before the foundation of the world, You set out a unique plan for my life.
What would my husband/wife see in me? ⇨⇨ Thank You, Lord Jesus, that my worth is secure in You.
I'll never measure up. ⇨⇨ Father, thank You that my value has nothing to do with what I do or don't do.
I'll never be good enough. ⇨⇨ Thank You, Father, that my worth is found in You.

I once heard someone say that before you allow a thought to be planted in your heart, inject the phrase "in Christ" in it and see if it makes sense. If the sentence doesn't make sense, toss it out. For example, "I'm a loser *in Christ*." That clearly doesn't line up with truth, so therefore toss it out by saying, "I rebuke that thought in the name of Jesus."

If you notice, casting down the negative thought has nothing to do with trying to prove yourself or who you are; rather, it asserts the truth about who God is, which lets the powers of darkness know *whom* your confidence is tied to. No need to get into a battle with the enemy, trying to prove who you are. Focus on getting to know Your Father, clinging to Him, and through Him getting to know who you are. That way when the enemy tries to insert his two cents, you spot his deception, cast it down, and keep moving.

Don't be surprised the first few times you do this if the enemy comes back and says, "Do you really believe this garbage?" Recognize he is tempting you. Don't answer him. Resist him. He's not worth your time. If anything, start praising the Lord for who He is, or turn on praise and worship music. He will flee because he can't stand an environment where God is glorified.

Chosen by God

You, my friend, have been chosen by God out of His goodness and love for you—specifically you. In His love God pursued you and made you His, and in His love He saved you. Just as He delivered the Israelites out of the hands of the Egyptians, in Christ, He delivered you out of the hands of the original narcissist, Satan. If He did that, He's more than able to deliver you out of the hands of one of Satan's little puppets, whether they're demons or living, breathing narcissists he tries to use in your life.

God knows exactly where you are, how you are, and how to lead you. During the exodus, there was a time when God chose to take the Israelites through a certain route rather than a shorter route. Exodus 13:17–18 says, "For God said, 'If they face war, they might change their minds and return to Egypt.' So God led the people around by the desert road toward the Red Sea." Your responsibility is to trust Him.

As a child of God, you have to understand that God is your Deliverer. He meets you where you are; He knows exactly what you need. Your healing journey may be different from your friends'—just as the Israelites' journey was different from the one the woman at the well experienced, and her journey was different from that of the demon-possessed man at the tombs of Gadara. But the Deliverer remains the same—the great I Am.

Your enemy will never stop trying to attack you as a child of God. One of the reasons the Israelites kept falling over and over is that they couldn't see past the bondage mindset. After God set them free, they continued to see themselves as slaves rather than children. They wanted someone to attach themselves to when the Lord had already claimed them. They wanted someone to give them worth when the Lord had already called them chosen.

If you feel as if your life is a series of mistakes caught in a revolving door, remember,

> the Spirit you received does not make you slaves, so that you live in fear again; rather, the Spirit you received brought about your adoption to sonship. And by him we cry, "Abba, Father." The Spirit himself testifies with our spirit that we are God's children.
>
> —Romans 8:15–16

Staying on the offense of the enemy's attack on your mind relies heavily on the fact that you see yourself as a beloved child of God, whom God is committed to (Phil. 1:6). You must also see yourself as an image bearer of God, whom God has put here for His plans and purposes (Eph. 2:10).

The basis of your identity has to be founded on the fact that you are loved by God. When you think of yourself, make "I am loved" the first description you use to describe yourself. And understand that you are loved not on the basis of what you could do but because you have an unchanging, faithful, loving, sovereign Father who chose you before the foundations of the world. Before you were ever born, God decided you were going to be His and that He would pursue you and love you and that your identity would become that of His beloved child.

When you hold on to your identity as God's beloved child, and the enemy comes whispering lies in your ear or uses a narcissist to spew poison in your mind, you'll be able to recognize, "Hey, this is not congruent with who I am, and therefore I will not accept it."

As a counselor, I can testify that it's not so much what people say to us that matters (although words have the power to pierce us); it's whether we choose to listen to those words. To listen means hearing and acting upon what we heard. That's why your enemy loves attacking you when you don't know who you are, because if you don't know that you are God's beloved child, he'll have a field day with you.

Like the example of the little child who believed he was bad just because his friend said he was, if you don't latch on to your Father's garment and let Him fill you with your true identity in Him, you'll receive anything Satan says to you about yourself. But when you filter everything the enemy whispers into your mind—whether via thoughts or what other people say—through the truth of God's Word, and through your identity as God's beloved child, you'll be surprised at how many thoughts and words will stop affecting you.

Do your absolute best to filter your thoughts through "I am God's beloved child"! If the thought contradicts that identity, don't entertain it—bring it before God and let His Word guide you. For example, when the enemy whispers to you in the first person, "I'm the worst," or "I'm such a loser," say out loud, "No, I'm God's beloved child. Thank You, Lord, for the way You love me."

Knowing Your True Identity Dissipates Anxiety

Knowing your identity as God's beloved child also has another amazing benefit: It dissipates anxiety rooted in fear of the unknown. As I'm writing this book, I have a doctor's appointment to check a spot in my body that seems questionable. And I can attest that had this happened ten years ago, I would have been beside myself waiting to go see the doctor. I would have lost sleep over it.

Ten years ago I still struggled with anxiety, especially when it came to the unknown that affected my life. My anxiety was through the roof. That's one of the reasons

I questioned whether God was calling the right person into the counseling field when I felt a pull toward it. In my mind not only was I unqualified to treat anxiety, but I hadn't yet figured out the road map myself to overcoming it. But thanks be to God, He doesn't leave us there, right? Throughout the years of counseling training, God incorporated His Word to train me.

The Bible says to let the Word of God dwell in you richly (Col. 3:16). That's not so we gain the most information about the Bible but because the more God's Word is in us, the more of a protective barrier we have against enemy deception. As I wait for my doctor's appointment, when the enemy tries to sneak in and whisper things to induce fear and anxiety, I don't even let him finish his sentence. I start praising the Lord for His faithfulness and thanking God for how much He loves me, regardless of any circumstances on the outside. And as I talk to the Lord and thank Him, I promise you, fear dissipates.

First Samuel 30:6 says, "David strengthened himself in the Lord" (ESV). David wasn't perfect; in fact, his mistakes and even full-fledged sins were out in the open, but his legacy is still that of a man after God's own heart—which goes to show that setting our identity on the fact that we are God's beloved children doesn't mean we're going to be perfect. What it does mean, however, is that the doubt the enemy whispers in our minds or the things he sends our way to try to destroy us won't be possible because greater is the Spirit of God who is in us than the enemy who is attacking us (1 John 4:4).

Friend, pay attention to the way you talk to yourself.

When you mess up, do you run to the Father, fall flat on your face before Him, ask for His forgiveness, and then ask Him to help you turn your back on the sin? Or do you run away from God in shame and try to overcorrect it? If you do the latter, I encourage you to step into your birthright and start practicing the former.

Stepping into your birthright in this situation means applying Hebrews 4:16: "Let us then approach God's throne of grace with confidence, so that we may receive mercy and find grace to help us in our time of need." Because then, and only then, will you experience the assurance that comes from knowing your Father sees everything about you. Yet He chose you out of His own will and is committed to loving you and sanctifying you little by little. That assurance is what brings us joy.

Joy comes from within. It is a state of being that is birthed out of full assurance of knowing that no matter what's going on out there, I know my Redeemer lives, and I know that I am His and He is mine. I know He loves me. I know He takes care of me. I know He's thinking about me even right now. And one day when I take my last breath, I know He will be the One to receive me into glory. That, my friend, is joy. Nothing in this world can give us joy. The world, including people, were never meant to be the source of our joy. Joy is a fruit of the Holy Spirit and therefore can only come from fellowship and intimacy with Him. Joy is not something we can strive for, work for, or earn; it is something God gives us out of His free will. It is one of His gifts to you, His beloved child.

As I was writing this book, I experienced a stressful work-related situation I had to handle the next day. Typically, when something like this happens, the enemy attacks my sleep and keeps me up thinking about what I'm going to say and how I'm going to handle it, preplanning the conversation, and so forth. The night before I had to deal with this issue, before I even closed my eyes, I asked the Lord to wake me up feeling refreshed before my alarm went off so I wouldn't get startled.

The next morning, as I squinted my eyes to see what time it was, I realized the Lord had woken me up fifteen minutes before my alarm was scheduled to go off. What an answered prayer! Not only that, but once I woke up and saw what time it was, I felt such joy knowing that my Father was right there with me, to the point where He answered a prayer I had specifically asked for. So I said, "Thank You, Father." Immediately, I felt the Lord respond in my spirit, "You're welcome ________________," referring to me using a word in my native language, Arabic—an endearing word He used at a time when I needed to hear it most, which meant "my beloved."

That whole day strengthened me from the inside out. It gave me such joy that the situation that normally would have caused me undue stress and sleepless nights barely phased me. I held on to the fact that no matter what was going on all around me, my Father was with me, and He calls me His beloved. That was all I needed to know to make it through my day with joy.

As I was writing this section of the book, the Lord brought that morning back to mind. I believe He wants you to hold on to that same truth—that regardless of what your situation looks like on the outside or how you feel on the inside, your Father is with you right now. The reason we go back to our old ways and risk falling back into the trap of narcissistic abuse is that we doubt God's presence. The enemy wants us to doubt the reality that God is actively pursuing us, because he knows if we truly realize how much the Father loves us, it will be game over for him. If we want to shut the door to future narcissistic abuse, we have to take inventory of our lives and ask the tough questions, such as, "How often do I *really* pause to seek my Father's presence? Do I seek His opinion before making a decision?"

In a world where everyone has an opinion about something, I dare you to pause and ask the Lord, the Prince of Peace, to give you His desires for your next step in life. I dare you to ask Him to remove any barriers that are keeping you from putting Him first and seeking His will first in your life. In a world where anxiety has dominated our mental health charts, I dare you to refuse to settle for anyone else's opinion until you seek the Father of wisdom—God.

That's how you shut the door to narcissistic abuse in the enemy's face. He won't be able to wiggle his way in to give you his opinion or use one of his puppets to do his bidding. Why? Because you've settled in your mind and determined in your heart that you will only take the step your Father has ordained for you—not because you're trying to earn His acceptance but because you know beyond a shadow of a doubt that in Christ you are His beloved.

Chapter 12

LIVING BLESSED

IT'S INCREDIBLE HOW God's timing works. Every year I set a goal to read my Bible from beginning to end. The night before I was going to start working on this chapter, I read Numbers 22–25. These three chapters of the Bible tell of a king by the name of Balak. This Moabite king had heard about how the Lord, who had previously delivered the Israelites out of the grip of mighty Pharaoh, had also given the Israelites victory over other nations, and he became afraid of what they might do to his own nation.

Determined he was not going to lose to the Israelites, he sought a plan to weaken them. King Balak summoned some of his officials and gave them money to find and pay off a prophet named Balaam, saying,

> A people has come out of Egypt; they cover the face of the land and have settled next to me. Now come and put a curse on these people, because they are too powerful for me. Perhaps then I will be able to defeat them and drive them out of the

> land. For I know that whoever you bless is blessed, and whoever you curse is cursed.
>
> —NUMBERS 22:5–6

King Balak sought to put a curse on the Israelites because he thought if they were under a curse, they would be weakened, and therefore he would be able to defeat them. Did you catch the word *defeat*? Doesn't that cycle sound familiar? Balak knew that the Israelites belonged to God because God's presence was very evident in their lives. Balak's plan was to make sure the Israelites didn't overpower him or take authority over him, and he thought by cursing them they wouldn't be able to. Unfortunately for him, when the officials reached the prophet, Balaam sought the Lord, and God said to him, "Do not go with them. You must not put a curse on those people, because *they are blessed*." So Balaam declined King Balak's offer and sent the elders on their way back.

Well, King Balak was not going to take no for an answer. Determined to bring defeat on the Israelites, He sent another group of officials who were "more numerous and more distinguished than the first" (Num. 22:15). The officials came to Balaam and said, "This is what Balak son of Zippor says: Do not let anything keep you from coming to me, because I will reward you handsomely and do whatever you say. Come and put a curse on these people for me" (vv. 16–18).

Balaam ended up meeting up with the Moabite king. Balak instructed Balaam to curse the Israelites. After seeking the Lord again, Balaam answered, "How can I curse those whom God has not cursed? How can I denounce those whom the Lord has not denounced?" (23:8). During their exchange, King Balak's plan backfired on him and Balaam ended up pronouncing blessings over the very people he was called to curse. This made King Balak very angry. As a result, he refused to compensate the prophet for coming and instead blamed God for not compensating him, saying, "The Lord has kept you from being rewarded" (24:11). Doesn't that sound like how a narcissist would twist the facts?

As I read this passage, I felt deep within my spirit that not only is this true about the Israelites, but it is true of you and me as well.

There's a lot of noise out there that tries to convince you that Satan or his demons can curse you even as God's child. That, my friend, is not biblical. You can see right here from God's Word that the devil and his demons cannot curse you, even if they summoned all their powers combined—not because you're powerful, not because you're great, not because you're smart, not because you're pretty, but because as God's child you have been set apart by Him. As His child you have the Holy Spirit of the living God dwelling on the inside of you, marking you as His, and therefore the devil cannot curse whom God has declared blessed.

Now pay attention. Just because Satan can't curse you directly doesn't mean he can't *deceive* you. Remember, when God made Adam and Eve, Genesis 1:28 says, "God blessed them." But by choosing to go against God's command, they brought a curse upon themselves.

As God's child living under the new covenant, you are also blessed. Galatians 3:13–15 (emphasis added) says it this way:

> Christ redeemed us from the curse of the law by becoming a curse for us, for it is written: "Cursed is everyone who is hung on a pole." He redeemed us in order that *the blessing* given to Abraham might come to the Gentiles through Christ Jesus, so that by faith we might receive the promise of the Spirit.

Since Satan can't curse you directly, he uses another avenue.

When King Balak refused to compensate Balaam, Balaam found another way to bring a curse on the Israelites. Balaam knew that the Israelites' blessing was directly tied to their reverence for and obedience to God. He knew that if he could get them to sin against God, they would end up bringing *a curse on themselves.* So he counseled the Moabites to entice the Israelites to "step out" on their relationship with God. Once the Israelites did, they bore the consequences of their actions.

Similar to how Satan deceived the Israelites, Satan, the original narcissist, will make every effort to deceive you. He knows that the way to bring destruction into your life is by getting you to turn away from God. In 1 Corinthians 10:1–6, Paul uses the failings of the Israelites to issue this warning to us:

> For I do not want you to be ignorant of the fact, brothers and sisters, that our ancestors were all under the cloud and that they all passed through the sea. They were all baptized into Moses in the cloud and in the sea. They all ate the same spiritual food and drank the same spiritual drink; for they drank from the spiritual rock that accompanied them, and that rock was Christ. Nevertheless, God was not pleased with most of them; their bodies were scattered in the wilderness. Now these things occurred as examples to keep us from setting our hearts on evil things as they did.

We set our hearts on evil things when we sway from our full allegiance to God. Paul continues in verses 11–12:

> These things happened to them as examples and were written down as warnings for us, on whom the culmination of the ages has come. So, if you think you are standing firm, be careful that you don't fall!

How do you make sure you don't fall? Don't put your hope in anyone or anything but God! He alone is worthy of your allegiance and praise. And remember, whatever and whoever your enemy tries to put in front of you is worthless in comparison with the Lord Jesus Christ.

Jesus is the most valuable person ever. Your value comes from Him, so no one else can take it away or influence it. In Christ, God has declared you blessed. I love the Hebrew translation of Psalm 91:14. It says, "Because he hath set his love upon me, therefore will

I deliver him: I will set him on high, because he hath known my name." When you determine to set your love on God and pursue Him with all your might, God will save you in times of trouble, and when temptations come your way, He will place you out of reach of your enemies and honor you. What a promise to hold on to!

Final Encouragement

I want to encourage you to not only use the steps we went over one time and forget them. Rather, make a habit of going through them quarterly to make sure you're not derailing in any area of your life. Watch out for idols, and again, by idols I don't mean golden calves; I mean anyone or anything that may draw your attention or time away from God.

Watch out for offense. The enemy will put someone in your life to offend you so that you can carry resentment, and as a result, he gets a foothold in your life (Eph. 4:26–27). When someone offends you, remember, don't take the bait! Choose to forgive. You are blessed regardless of what that person has called you or done to you. Your worth is not measured by how they treated you but by who God declared you to be.

Watch out for inner vows you make, and make sure you especially pay attention to the "I'll never" or "I'll always" phrases you think or speak. Let the fear of the Lord lead you—meaning, value God more than you value anyone or anything in your life, and keep your allegiance to Him alone. Pursue Him with everything you have.

Remember that no matter what you are facing in this life, and who you're facing, nothing and no one comes close to the sovereignty of God, and if you're submitted to Him, no matter how the enemy decides to use that person, or how invested the powers of darkness are in your situation, praise the Lord through it and trust that *He is your Deliverer.*

This is why when you speak God's truth about you, those affirmations have to begin with "*In Christ, I am ________________.*" This not only serves as a reminder to you but is a declaration to the kingdom of darkness that you have been paid for, redeemed, justified, and spiritually healed, and that you know it, believe it, and stand on that truth as well. Because of this you don't have to listen to the enemy's accusations or to the accusations and condemnations Satan throws your way using one of his puppets.

You also don't have to heed his enticement. When Satan tries to get you to befriend your boss so you might have favor with them and maybe get that promotion you've been wanting, as soon as the thought comes to mind, don't entertain it. Turn away from it because you already have the favor of the Lord, and if the Lord wants you to get that promotion, trust and believe you *will* get that promotion.

When Satan entices you to flex your power to try to prove how valuable you are, how smart you are, how good you are at something, or even how good-looking you are, resist him, brother or sister in the faith. And say out loud: "I have been crucified with Christ, and I no longer live, but Christ lives in me. The life I now live in the body, I live by faith in the Son of God, who loved me and gave himself for me" (Gal. 2:20).

Never ever compromise your time with the Lord, because He is the most important person in your life, whether or not you realize it. The longer you spend time with Him and invest your time with Him, the more you'll realize it. Last, and certainly not least, understand that your value comes from being made in God's image and through Christ, belonging to God, who is worthy beyond measure. Don't fall for the enemy's tricks to get you to earn your value by over-accommodating, prove your value by rebelling, or seek your value by acting in arrogance, or make you believe you're unworthy through self-defeat. All those are lies because you are a child of God, and in Christ, Your Father has declared you valuable.

A PERSONAL INVITATION TO KNOW JESUS

God loves you deeply. His Word is filled with promises that reveal His desire to bring healing, hope, and abundant life to every area of your being—body, mind, and spirit. More than anything, He wants a personal relationship with you through His Son, Jesus Christ.

If you've never invited Jesus into your life, you can do so right now. It's not about religion—it's about a relationship with the One who knows you completely and loves you unconditionally. If you're ready to take that step, simply pray this prayer with a sincere heart:

> *Lord Jesus, I want to know You as my Savior and Lord. I confess and believe that You are*

> *the Son of God and that You died for my sins. I believe You rose from the dead and are alive today. Please forgive me for my sins. I invite You into my heart and my life. Make me new. Help me to walk with You, grow in Your love, and live for You every day. In Jesus' name, amen.*

If you just prayed that prayer, you've made the most important decision of your life. All of heaven rejoices with you, and so do I! You are now a child of God, and your journey with Him has just begun. Please contact my publisher at pray4me@charismamedia.com so that we can send you some materials that will help you become established in your relationship with the Lord. We look forward to hearing from you.

ACKNOWLEDGMENTS

I'M GRATEFUL TO the Lord God, our great Deliverer—Jesus Christ. Thank You, Holy Spirit of the living God, for guiding me through this process. I'm grateful to the love of my life, David, for his constant support through each assignment the Lord calls me to; to our children, Benjamin and Eliza, for the childlike faith they demonstrate to me daily; to the Charisma team for partnering with me to bring this project to fruition; and to my lovely editor, Angie Kiesling, for her time, effort, and dedication to this book. To God be the glory.

NOTES

Chapter 2

1. Yu L. L. Luo, Huajian Cai, and Hairong Song, "A Behavioral Genetic Study of Intrapersonal and Interpersonal Dimensions of Narcissism," *PLOS One* 9, no.4 (April 2, 2014): e93403, https://doi.org/10.1371/journal.pone.0093403.
2. Allen G. Ross et al., "Adverse Childhood Experiences Leading to Narcissistic Personality Disorder: A Case Report," *BMC Psychiatry* 24 (November 22, 2024): article 842, https://doi.org/10.1186/s12888-024-06307-9.

ABOUT THE AUTHOR

KENZA HADDOCK, LPCS, BCPC, is a licensed professional counselor supervisor and a board-certified pastoral counselor. A former Muslim, Haddock was called by God when she had a dream about Jesus. The experience was so profound she left Islam and became an ambassador for Christ. Haddock is a certified clinical trauma professional. She and her husband own Oceanic Counseling Group LLC, an outpatient mental health agency headquartered in South Carolina. Haddock has been featured on over one hundred media outlets, including *Life Today* with Randy Robison, *The Basement* with Tim Ross, and Christian television networks, for her expertise in Christian counseling. Her published works include *The Three Enemies of Your Mental Health*, *The Ex-Muslim's Guide to Christianity*, and *Your 3 Inherent Needs*.

JOURNAL YOUR THOUGHTS